One Heart at a Time

Jesus' Simple Plan to Transform the World

Ron Johnson

2st Edition

D1167188

I want to share a little story with you. In April of 2011 while having Coffee Time With Jesus I ask Jesus this question.

Jesus when the apostles ask "how do we pray?" you gave them the amazing Our Father Prayer; so dearest Jesus I would like a prayer from you; that when I say it everyone in heaven will rejoice. My Jesus is so kind to me; He even made the prayer rim so I could remember it easier. Here is the prayer Jesus gave me.

Dearest heavenly Father; In Jesus name I pray;
As I walk down the street today
I pray the people I see along the way,
When they get home tonight and start to pray.
Will say: I think I saw Jesus today.

Table of Contents

Short Message

The intention of Jesus and I for writing this book is to encourage everyone to transform the hearts of people around you, *one heart at a time*. Just put all your faith, hope and trust to Jesus, and He will make a difference. I'm also inviting everyone to make yourself available to Him – go and please ask Him, *'Jesus, what are we going to do today?'* I tell you that all things are possible for those who believe in the love of Jesus to transform hearts.

If this book made an impact in your life, I invite you to call me at 513 377-1727. Transform the world, one heart at a time by simply being the love of my Jesus!

Jenny, Ron and Jesus will love you now and forever!

www.CoffeeTimeWithJesus.com
513-377-1727

One Heart at a Time

It was February 09, almost five years ago when my wife Jenny and I started an adventure to live for God and go wherever God needed us to go. God responded by opening His doors for us to share His love everywhere. I don't ask for signs and wonders to follow. I just follow Jesus and I don't pray asking Jesus where should I go or what should I do. I know Jesus called us to follow Him so I just go and I know by faith if I am going the wrong way my Lord will turn me around.

Last year, I was in Northern OH visiting friends when another friend, Joel Sweeney from Cincinnati called and asked me if I wanted to join his team and go to Detroit, MI. I was thrilled and saw his request as a great honor. Joel goes around the world, helping people by preaching God's Word and letting God perform miracles through him everywhere He goes. The timing of his request was great and I was honored to be part of God's team, so I went.

I picked a campground on the south side of Detroit and set up a day ahead of their arrival. Although they were coming from the south also, Joel's team stayed at a motel on the north side of Detroit. We met and went into the center of downtown to do some street ministry. It turns out the Detroit baseball team won a game that night so there was a festive mood. The people of Detroit we saw were pretty drunk or high on drugs. The bars were packed and rocking and rolling. As some of the team members were street ministering to people I realized this type of ministry was not my cup of tea. I could not hear what the team was praying for or the responses of the person being prayed for. The background noise was too much for my ears.

I stepped away from the team and as I was watching the people in the bars screaming for joy about their team winning a baseball game, I felt overwhelmed and powerless to change this mess. The devil and his drugs and his juice were flowing everywhere. It seemed that I had walked into the devil's own yard.

As I observed, I saw the people were so messed up. I'm sure the devil was alive and well there. I'm sure the devil was very pleased looking at all the people who are listening to him. I mean, there was a guy alongside of me lying on the sidewalk passed out and you could see he was so drunk that he lost control of his urine and had already soaked himself. I wanted to run into the bar and jump up on the table and tell these lost souls, "You want something to scream for joy about? Jesus came and died for you all!" but I felt no release from my Jesus to do that.

I felt so overwhelmed, as I stood on the street looking at all the drunken people in the bars. Thank God, I know who has the answer so I just went right to my source and ask my Jesus, "How do we change this mess? I mean there are thousands of people here." Right in the middle of all that noise I heard from my Jesus and as usual Jesus answered my question with a question, "How did I tell you to minister Ron?" I answered "Jesus you told me, *one heart at a time.*" But I was so overwhelmed that I ask Jesus again saying, "Lord there are so many people here, how can one heart at a time make an inroad in this mess?" My Jesus is so patient with me and answered with the same question "Ron, how did I teach you to make a difference?" I said "Okay Jesus. One heart at a time." Then, I rejoined the team as we ministered one heart at a time.

That night, the team went back to their motel and we pulled our money so we could buy hotdogs and food to feed the hungry in the inner city that Saturday. The team found an empty field alongside a building called the NSO building. A pastor named Jim was on the team and brought a big grill to cook with. The field was a mess, but we managed to set up the grill and a table to serve on. People started coming to eat; Jim also had a P.A. system to talk on, so he could preach to the people as we fed them. I was totally taken back again by the living conditions of the homeless there. My heart was breaking and yet the team was ministering in the power of God. I knew my God will make a difference in the life of these homeless persons. After we packed up, we went to another place that night to street minister.

We also decided to pull our money and feed the hungry again the next morning. Because the team was staying on the north side of town and I was camping on the south side of town, I realized I didn't need to go all the way up north to meet them. We were going to the same field by the NSO building so I told them I'll just meet them there.

The next morning, I arrived an hour or so ahead of the team, so I decided to go into the alleys and abandoned buildings to tell the homeless people we were going to feed them at 11 A.M. I gently woke them up and told them that we are going to feed them again. I saw how they sleep on a piece of cardboard or just in the dirt. Their living conditions are so hard to witness and my heart was aching to do more than to feed them. I asked my Jesus what He wanted to say to them and how could our team encourage them.

Jesus started speaking to me! After an hour or so, I went back to the field again and saw that the team had arrived. They were standing by my car and looked puzzled. When they saw me, a girl named Lisa who was one of the team came running and hugged me. You see, in my desire to tell the people about the food we had for them, I forgot to close my car door. Also, the windows of my car were still rolled down because my air conditioning does not work, they saw my keys were on the floor and the GPS was still on the windshield. The puzzled look on the faces of the team disappeared when they saw me and as they told me they could not figure out what had happened to me.

As we started feeding the hungry, Jim got on the tailgate of his truck and was preaching on Ephesians 3:20 that God will do exceedingly above all you can ask. After he finished, Pastor Jim asked if anyone else wanted to talk to these people. So I jumped up on the tailgate and spoke the words Jesus gave me to speak. As Jesus spoke through me to the crowd, I realized they were all staring at me. Even the people serving food stopped serving and were listening. My Jesus is so powerful! He touched a lot of hearts that morning.

I believe a lot of hearts received hope that morning and the people who received the hope of Jesus where feed both spiritually and physically. With the love of Jesus in their heart, I know and I believe that their life will be impacted. Then, I jumped down off the tailgate and went back to serve food. As each person came by me, I blessed them and they received the blessing. Some of the people I blessed said to me "you are the blessing" I replayed, no sir I can feed you today but my Jesus can feed you for eternity if you just don't give up hope in Him. My Jesus gave Hope for the hopeless and love for the ones that might have thought no one loved them. And that is the most powerful message of hope and love anyone can receive from my Jesus.

As we were packing up, the team asked me to go out to eat with them. I arrived at the restaurant a couple minutes after everyone else. So they were waiting on the sidewalk as I got out of my car. I heard them laughing as I was rolling up the windows of my car. I turned around and asked them what's so funny. They answered, "*You!* Because when you were in the worst part of town you left your windows down and your car doors open. Now that we are in the nice part of town, you rolled your windows up!" I smiled and said, "My Jesus protects me where ever I go. I just thought it might rain."

A couple of weeks later, I was in Pittsburg, PA. I met some friends there and one of them used to sell insurance. After dinner he gave me a hypothetical question: He asked me to work for him 30 days at 8 hours a day. He offered me one of two pay scales. First is 50 dollars per hour, which equals to $12,000 or he would pay me a penny the first day, and double it every day for thirty days. The first day I would have a penny, the second I would have two pennies and the third day 4 pennies, etc. Then he asked me which pay scale I would want. I answered that I would take the $12,000. He replied that most people would pick the same, but they would be leaving over 5 million dollars behind. Yes, a penny doubled every day for just 30 days equals 5,368,709.00 dollars. He started showing me this on his calculator, and as I watched the numbers jumping on the screen, I heard my Jesus say, "Ron, that is your *one heart at a time.*"

My spirit jumped inside of me for I suddenly knew that I, Ron Johnson, can change the world. There is nothing I cannot do. All things are possible for those who believe in the love of Jesus to transform hearts. I believe Jesus loves Ron Johnson and I know I have the love of Jesus in me. So together, Jesus and I will transform the heart of one person today. We (Jesus and I) will see the world transformed one heart at a time.

I don't need some big organization. I don't need computers. I don't need any material things. I have Jesus living inside of me so I simply ask my Jesus, "What are we going to do today?" Pretty simple isn't it? WHAT ARE WE GOING TO DO TODAY, JESUS? Now I know how one heart at a time works. THANK YOU JESUS! That is the good news of the gospel! Now that's my Jesus!

Here is a simple way to start your day: JUST ASK JESUS "WHAT ARE WE GOING TO DO TODAY?"

By asking Jesus, "What are we going to do today?" I am making myself available to my Jesus! I am allowing Jesus to use me all day and every day. I really want to be used by Jesus and yet, Jesus almost never answers this question. So how do I know Jesus hears me? By faith I know Jesus hears me so I go about my day as usual. If I need to repair something on the camper or go to the grocery store, I just do whatever I think needs to be done. I talk with my Jesus all day long for I know He is with me all day long. After dedicating the day to Jesus, the most important thing I can do is make sure I have a lot of quiet time so I can hear My Jesus.

Almost everyday something comes up like I see someone in need of help or maybe someone that just looks lonely. Whatever Jesus has for me to do, He knows that I am available. Then, at the end of the day I simply rest knowing I have made myself available to my Jesus. I let Jesus set the goals and I rest knowing He hears me and I rest knowing Jesus loves me! The peace of Jesus is priceless.

AN ENCOUNTER AT A STORE

One day I went to a camper store to buy some rubber roof coating. The salesman showed me the different types of coatings and helped me make an informed decision on the products. While talking to him, I sensed that he was depressed, so I asked him if

13

something was wrong. He looked at me and almost started crying right there in the store. He told me he feels his boss was trying to fire him because he had less than a year to his retirement. He also said that if he gets fired, he will lose his pension and that would save the company a lot of money.

I put my hand on his shoulder and prayed for peace in his life and for his boss to find real ways to save the company money. I prayed for his boss to acknowledge him above his own expectation! The salesman thanked me for praying for Him.

As he rang up my merchandise, he gave me the total of $39.48. I was surprised and said, "I think something is wrong. I thought the roof coating alone cost $109.00." He checked and said that I was correct and he fixed the computer error right away. I also gave this man some papers Jesus and I wrote, one of them is called *Coffee Time With Jesus*. I have my phone number written on these papers and I told him if he had any comments he could call me.

The following Monday, I received a call from the same store clerk. He said he was on the way into work that morning and he was crying out to the Lord, asking Jesus to let him know what to do to keep from being fired. He felt for some reasons that he was going to be fired that day. He actually cried knowing his pension was going to disappear and how that would affect his retirement. At his place of employment you do not punch a time clock you simply go to your workstation and start the computer cash register.

He had only logged in a couple minutes when his boss called him into his office. He said his heart sank as he walked to the office. He said he prayed out loud *"please Lord, help me!"* as he entered the office to find his boss and supervisor there. He said he could not see the ax in their hands, but he felt he was going to be chopped up and kicked out.

His boss told him when they installed the new computer cash registers a little over a year ago and there was a tracking system installed also. After a year of monitoring the entire counter staff, they realized he was their most valuable employee. The boss added that he has the best customer relations, which he found the most computer errors, and he had the highest number of customers waited on etc. He was the best counterman they had and they gave him a huge bonus.

At lunch time he went to his truck and prayed to Jesus, thanking Him and all of a sudden he felt a huge desire to buy a cup of coffee and give it to Jesus. After calling to tell me the good news, He also invited Jenny and I to come to his church and meet his family. We did and found that they were wonderful people.

DRIVING DOWN THE ROAD

I had another encounter about a couple of weeks ago. I was asked to speak at a college in Tennessee. I was asked be there by eleven o'clock. While on my way to the college, a car passed me on a four-lane highway. I noticed there was steam coming out from under the car and it seemed that the driver didn't realize he had a problem. I caught up with his car and got alongside. I started making signs for him to pull over, but he was reluctant to pull over. But for some reason, he did slow down and I got in front of him and he did pull over.

I ran back to his car and told him there was steam blowing under his car and his car was overheating. With his window still up and the door locked, he checked his temperature gauge and replied that his car is not overheating. All of the sudden, the steam started coming up around the hood and he realized that I was telling the truth.

He opened the hood and we started looking for the leak. I said out loud, "Dear Jesus, show me something simple to fix!" The leak appeared to be coming from the water pump, but we needed to fill the radiator to be sure. So I went to my car because I know I carry an extra gallon of anti-freeze in my trunk. But when I reached for it, I saw that it was empty. I remembered I had used it to help someone in North Carolina last week and had not replaced it yet.

Thank God the man had some water in his car so we topped off the radiator. As he went to start the car I said out loud, "Dear Jesus, show us something simple to fix!" He started his car and we saw the leak was in a heater hose right above the water pump. It happens that I carry a small tool box in my trunk and as I was asking Jesus to help me fix the problem the man suddenly ask me,

"Who are you?" I just smiled back to him and replied that I am a believer in Jesus.

The man said he was not going to pull over, but when he slowed down, he saw my bumper sticker that says *Coffee Time With Jesus*. He thought to himself the bumper sticker says *'Jesus'* so he thought this is going to be okay. It turned out Jesus did show me something simple: the heater hose had a pin hole in it. The pin hole was spraying the leak right on the water pump, so it appeared to be the pump.

I cut the hose and stretched it enough to reconnect it. All I needed to finish the repair was a special hose clamp, so I prayed out loud to Jesus for the hose clamp. The man was standing alongside the car and asked where are you going to find a clamp like that around here. I turned around to look in my tool box, and right in the top tray was the clamp that I needed. The hose stretched enough to reconnect and with this hose clamp tightened, I topped off the radiator, tested it for leaks and found none so off he went.

I was a half hour late getting to college, but everything worked out great there also. There was not a formal meeting place like with a guest speaker so I just spoke in a lounge as people came and went all day. The really cool part was some of the young students stayed and listened all day and into the night. One of the young men that stayed all day asked me a question. He said, "Ron, all these testimonies are from the past, I would like to know what God has done through you today? You know what I mean? Has Jesus given you anything to do this morning?" I smiled and told Him about the car that had steam coming from under it.

Just make yourself available to my Jesus and when something pops up, pull over and help. Jesus never passed up anyone and neither should we. Doing the will of the Father really is that simple. A good friend of mine, Todd White put it this way: Show me one person Jesus did not die for and I won't pray for that one.

When you truly know that Jesus lives inside of you, your life changes from *'what do I want to do today?'* to *'what does Jesus need me to do today?'* I love my very best friend Jesus, but knowing my best friend loves me is revelation that takes fear and puts it in the rear vision mirror. Jesus said that His perfect love cast out fear and I believe Jesus.

One heart at a time works when you trust God to bring the increase. Please don't ever think you don't make a difference because to Jesus you are the difference. We are to be His love.

Perfect Love

1 John 4:18 There is no fear in love; but perfect love casts out fear, because fear involves torment. But he who fears has not been made perfect in love.

Perfect love! Who among us is perfect in anything? Yet to have the Perfect love of Jesus in us must be possible for Jesus said so. Understanding the perfect love of our Father and Jesus has for us is great revelation. This revelation is so important to removing fear. Fear really is nothing more than doubting in the love of our Father and Jesus to take care of us. To understand the perfect love of Jesus we must understand that Jesus loved us even in our sin. I believe we can have the perfect love of Jesus in us and so I have His perfect love in me! Please believe to receive.

I see so many people trying to love Jesus. They are trying to be good enough to be loved by Jesus. That is backwards! They feel a need to perform for God to prove they are good Christians. All you need to do to please God is to have faith in His Word. How many Christians do you know that will not pray for someone to be healed? Although they will bring a sick person a bowl of soup and pray for the doctor to do a good job and the whole time they are thinking that they are doing the right thing and they are. Which among these takes more faith? Praying for the doctor to do a good job or praying to God for healing? I believe the perfect love of Jesus is to heal everyone.

Hebrews 11:6 But without faith it is impossible to please Him, for he who comes to God must believe that He is, and that He is a rewarder of those who diligently seek Him.

Diligently seek God by asking Him, "What are we going to do today?" Diligently seek God by believing His word is true. Diligently seek God by simply listening to His voice and asking for discernment. Diligently seek God by spending time reading His bible, His manual for receiving His perfect love in your heart.

1 John 4:19 We love Him, because He first loved us.

The concept of Jesus loving us first seems to be very hard for some people to understand. I know it was true for me. I was taught from my youth that I am a sinner saved by grace. I was totally okay with that teaching because I knew I repented and I knew that I had a firm attitude not to sin anymore. The problem with the sinner saved by grace teaching is that I spent all my time trying not to sin and I never realized that I could have a relationship with Jesus. I was not taught to dwell on what is good. I ridiculously spent most of my time trying not to sin.

Trying not to sin makes you sin conscience. Being aware of sin or trying not to sin by thinking all day (*I am not going to sin today*) puts your mind on the sin you are trying not to do. This type thinking will kill all of your efforts. It steals your joy because you feel like a failure when you do sin. Trying not to sin will destroy any relationship you have with God. I mean, after a while you start thinking why doesn't God help me? The real question should be *"why am I focused on sin instead of God?"* Now, because I read about the life of Jesus in the Bible, I know Jesus told us what to think on and I know Jesus focused on His relationship with His Father. Jesus never focused on sin or the devil.

Philippians 4:8 Finally, brethren, whatever things are true, whatever things are noble, whatever things are just, whatever things are pure, whatever things are lovely, whatever things are of good report, if there is any virtue and if there is anything praiseworthy — meditate on these things.

Do you see anywhere in this Scripture for us to think or focus on sin or for us to try not to sin by focusing on the sin you don't want to do? Jesus said what you think about is what you become. Sin is likened to a master. If you dwell on sin long enough, you will probably start to hate yourself because all you will see is the sin your in. Sin can rule your life and become like a master over you.

Matthew 6:24 No one can serve two masters; for either he will hate the one and love the other, or else he will be loyal to the one and despise the other. You cannot serve God and mammon.

You pray and ask God, *"Help me not to sin today."* You don't realize that you are already consumed with sin, guilt, shame, and condemnation. The worst part is you have no peace, no joy, no love, and eventually you might just give up and say this is just the way I am. You might even start to blame God saying why aren't you helping Lord?

Jesus says in Philippians:

Philippians 4:7 And the peace of God, which surpasses all understanding, will guard your hearts and minds through Christ Jesus.

Focus on Jesus, and the peace of God shall guard your hearts and minds through Christ Jesus. That sure doesn't sound sin conscious to me! We all want peace of mind and Jesus tells us we can have His peace which surpasses all our understanding. We can have this peace by keeping our hearts and our minds focused on Christ Jesus. Jesus is telling us the way not to sin is to keep our minds on Christ Jesus. Isn't that simple? Now, I wake up asking Jesus, *"What we are going to do today?"* I find myself thinking about Jesus and how much He loves me. John the apostle said numerous times, "I am the apostle Jesus loved".

Today, some people would call John conceited. I know how John felt. I have been criticized for calling Jesus 'my best friend'. I know Jesus sees something in me that is special and loveable. Jesus came to earth to show me how to please Him. I know Jesus will make us all feel this special but only if we let Him. That is why I tell everyone I am His favorite and I know Jesus loves me that much. Please take some time out of your busy day and listen to Jesus. Let Him talk to you and then let Jesus make you His favorite also. Stay Jesus conscious and the sins will run away!

When you know for a fact that Jesus loves you and you are his favorite, you will have peace that passes all understanding and you won't be sin conscious but you will be Jesus conscious. Jesus said for us to seek Him with all our heart, mind and spirit. Jesus is my best friend and I know it. He wants to be your best friend too, so make Him your best friend by simply asking Jesus into your heart and give Him some quiet time.

To really transform hearts to Jesus you must know how much Jesus loves you. Your life with Jesus in you will be such a shining example of the perfect love of Jesus. People will want what they see in you. Jesus said the eyes are a window to the soul. Be single-minded by seeking Jesus with your whole mind, body and soul. Seek Jesus with your whole heart! I simply make Jesus my treasure by giving Jesus my heart.

Matthew 6:21-22 For where your treasure is, there your heart will be also. The lamp of the body is the eye. If therefore your eye is good, your whole body will be full of light.

Don't let sin steal your joy and peace. You can only have joy and peace if you keep your focus on Jesus, for Jesus is your treasure and through knowing Him we receive joy and piece. We can only transform people, one heart at a time if we keep our focus on Jesus and have the Joy of the Lord in our heart. And through this Joy, people will see that you have Jesus and His perfect love will shine from your heart to theirs. The perfect love of Jesus in your heart shines through your Joy and will make them very eager to have this same Joy too!

Transformations

Not a long time ago, I was asked to go with the Go Network Team to Duluth Minnesota. After ministering all Saturday and into the night, we went to the motel after to get some rest. We were sitting in the lounge area talking about the great day we had when a young man came out of the bar pretty drunk. Some of the team tried to talk to him about God but he didn't want to listen. He said, "I will let God rescue me later. Right now I just want to be wild and crazy. I want to sow my wild oats and have fun." I just listened as some of the team tried to explain how knowing God will bring more joy into your life than all the wild and craziness could ever bring. He said, "I'm too young for God. I really like having wild and crazy in my life right now and besides I'm going to have a wild testimony someday when I let God rescue me."

Later, as I walked to my room, I kept thinking about the words of the drunken boy in the lounge. I asked my Jesus where this idea about how you will rescue him later comes from. It's almost like he needed to be wild and crazy, so Jesus could rescue him. The young man seemed to think this is normal and the right path to the Lord. The young man showed no remorse for the wild and crazy life he was living.

I didn't get an answer from Jesus that night but a couple of weeks later when I was in a church somewhere, I heard the pastor of the church giving his testimony about how wild and crazy he was when God rescued him out of the darkness. He even gave details no one needed to hear. Really, it sounded like he was bragging about how bad he was and how much fun he had. Right then I heard from my Jesus, "There is your answer Ron." The young man back in the lounge might have gone to that church as a child or heard preachers testimony's like that.

Jesus told us our words have meaning and we will be accountable for all our words. I believe in transformations, but not all transformations are from or to God. The word of our testimony is powerful. But if we concentrate on the wild and crazy part and not God and His love for us, we may be leading people astray instead of into His love.

I really think to transform a heart we need to simply let the love of God flow through us. I believe our testimony should be 99% glory to God and if need be to make the point 1% us. I hope this doesn't sound critical of the preacher or someone that has had a testimony like his. I pray for our testimonies to be informative. I pray for God to receive the glory from our testimony. If you are being convicted right now, please thank God for His gentle conviction, for I know for a fact the convicting of God is only with love and the convicting of God is so painless that we only see the results not the pain.

Who are we listening to and whose word are we spreading?

The other day I went to the store. While I was there, I picked up a sports drink they had on sale. On the way home, I drank one of the drinks. Shortly after arriving home, I noticed I was suffering from a headache. I prayed and it went away. Thank you Jesus! The next afternoon, I drank another sports drink and it tasted really good and had a nice flavor. Within a half hour I had another headache. I prayed and it went away. A couple of days later, I drank another sports drink and had another headache. It took me three headaches to realize I had a headache every time I drank one of the sport drinks. My first thought was I am going to throw the rest away.

Then I came to my senses and asked my source, Jesus, "Should I throw the rest away?" I heard from Jesus, "You didn't bless them." Immediately, I went to the refrigerator and blessed the sports drink and drank it. And if you guessed that I didn't get a headache, then you guessed right! My Jesus is so thoughtful and I am so blessed to have Him as my personal best friend.

A true transformation will lead you into an intimate relationship with my Jesus and you will ask Jesus everything. A transformed heart will hear His voice and the voice of the stranger it will not follow. I could have listened to the voice of the stranger and I would have probably told everyone, "Don't drink that sport drink, it will only give you a headache." You see, because of my intimate relationship with Jesus; Jesus makes my life simple and I am spreading His Word and not the words of the enemy.

Jesus is alive and real in a transformed heart. Knowing Jesus loves me makes my heart sing! The Joy of the Lord is real and more powerful than the depression of the enemy. I have the *joy, joy, joy down in my heart where down in my heart!* Yes! Rejoice and be glad for the Joy in the Lord is real and I did not get a headache!

DEDICATE YOUR LIFE TO JESUS

While I was at Duluth, MI, I met a guy named Jay Cole. This man knows a lot about making movies. He fell in love with Jenny's story and decided to film some of her story. One day we went out for a ride. Jay took me to a roadside park overlooking Lake Superior. He filmed me talking about my Jenny. When Jay was finished and as he was putting his stuffs away, I was walking around on the huge rocks that form the overlook.

Two young girls came walking by me and I just could not help but tell them how cute their smiles were. As I commented about their smile, their older sister walked up to us. I said, "Wow, you have the same beautiful smile as your younger sisters. You all have such beautiful eyes. You must know Jesus?" The little one came right back at me and said, "Yes, we know Jesus!" I asked, "Do you know what it means to dedicate your life to Jesus?"

The little one piped up again and said "Why don't you tell us?" Just as I started to tell them, their grandparents walked up towards us. Grandma took one look at me and wanted to know why an old man was talking to her grandchildren. She walked up and asked, "What is going on here?" The little girl looked at her grandma and said, "He is going to tell what it means to dedicate your life to Jesus." The grandmother said, "I would like to hear this." She looked at me and said, "Go ahead."

I continued, "For some people, when they think about dedicating their life to God, they think of Mother Teresa. They assume to dedicate your life to Jesus means you have to go to some foreign country and probably eat worms and live in total poverty.

Some people are called to live like that and it is a beautiful way to lay down their life for God. I have the most respect for Mother Teresa. She is a true example of dying to self that Jesus talks about in the Bible. Although most of the time, I believe God just wants us to be available to Him."

"You can dedicate your life to God by simply asking God every day, 'Dearest Jesus, what are WE going to do today?' By asking God this simple question, you are making yourself available to God to do whatever He needs you to do. When I ask God that question I almost never get an answer. So I just go about my day knowing God will put something in my path He needs done and Jesus knows I will make time to see it done." Just then, their grandma said, "I suppose you have an example?" To which I replied, "Yes, I do!"

I shared, "One day after asking God 'What are we going to do today' and not getting an answer, I dressed my Jenny and put her in the car so we could buy some groceries. Oh, I forgot to tell you about my Jenny. My wife Jenny was diagnosed with Pick's disease about sixteen years ago. Pick's disease attacks your brain and the brain dies. At the point of this story, Jenny was in a wheel chair and needed constant care."

I continued on with the story, "So we shopped and paid for our groceries. As I pushed my Jenny in the wheelchair to our car and pulled the grocery cart with my other hand, I noticed a man leaning against the front of the grocery store. He was all by himself and had a weird walker. The way he was leaning on the brick building alarmed me and I thought to myself that man needs some help."

"So I moved Jenny and the cart to a safe place by our car in the handicapped parking area. Then I ran about the 30 or 40 feet distance towards man and asked, 'Do you need some help?' The man started mumbling and made some noise. I realized that he could not talk. I thought to myself *Oh God, now what do I do?*"

"Just then, I noticed a young girl running towards me through the parking lot. As she got closer and our eyes met, she slowed down to let an older lady, which happens to be her grandma catch up. When grandma got close to me she said quite abruptly 'what are you doing?' I said 'I saw this man leaning against the front of this building and I thought he needed help'. Grandma said very sternly 'he doesn't need your help, he is with us'. I asked if she would mind if I pray for him.

"Immediately grandma melted right in front of me, her stern voice suddenly turned very sweet and kind as she said 'you want to pray for him?' To which I replied, 'yes I do'. She told me to pray for him almost like she just wanted to see what I would say."

"I put my hand on his shoulder and prayed. *Dear Heavenly Father I don't know what the spirit of infirmity is in this man but I know you do, so in the mighty name of Jesus Christ I command that spirit to go away.* As I prayed the man stared doing sign language, so I asked the grandma, *what did he say?*"

"She replied to me that he wants to know who I am. I told him that I am a believer in Jesus and I believe Jesus wants to lavish His love on you today. Just then, a big SUV pulled up alongside of us and they all started scurrying to get into the car. I thought to myself, *I guess I am done.*"

"I walked about 30 feet over to my Jenny and started to untie her from of the wheel chair. I opened the door to our car and picked Jenny up out of the wheelchair and put her in our car. Then I noticed someone standing behind me. I turned around to see the mother of the man whom I had prayed for, the driver of the SUV standing behind me."

"I saw her watery eyes as she said 'you don't know what you just did.' I replied 'you are right. I don't know what I just did.' She told me she was upset because while they were in the store shopping someone actually got mad at her son because he could not get out of their way fast enough. Again, I felt prompted by my Jesus so I said, "I don't believe Jesus wanted you to go home with that hurt tonight." With more tears in her eyes, she smiled and said 'you know I am not going home with that hurt tonight', and then she hugged me and drove away."

"So I finished putting the groceries in the car and buckled my little Jenny into her seat. When I got in the car, I just sat there talking to my Jesus telling Him how assuring He is. I praise you

Jesus for every breath I take and I love doing the work of your kingdom."

I told the girls, "It probably took me longer to convey this story to you than to actually live it. You see, that was all God had for me to do that day. I hope you could hear the joy in my heart as I told you the story because it brings joy to me every time Jesus reminds me of it."

The little girls were still smiling and the grandma said that was a great story. She wanted to know more about my Jenny and our journey. I said, "Jesus and I have actually written two books about my Jenny and our journey." We walked to my car and I gave them Jenny's books and we were all filled with the Joy of the Lord. I Thank you my Jesus for making your *joy my joy*!

Jesus Cleans Us Up

When I was young, I never thought I could be worthy of God's love because I thought I was a sinner saved by grace. I was never taught or even had a thought that I could be loved by God before I cleaned myself of all my sin issues. Can you imagine hearing loving parents say to their brand new baby, *"Now, clean yourself up and make yourself worthy and then we will love you!"* I know Jesus is the one who cleans us up! Jesus never told the apostles to go and clean themselves up and then come follow Him. Jesus asked the apostles to follow Him and Jesus is asking us to simply follow Him. For Jesus knows the steps to righteousness and Jesus knew His goodness will lead a man to repentance.

Accept the goodness of God in your heart today. Expect to follow in His footsteps today and be His ambassador through your loving example today. When trials come our way we will have the heart of Jesus in us and the mind of Jesus in us and the spirit of Jesus in us and we will know there is nothing impossible for us today.

Romans 2:4 Or do you despise the riches of His goodness, forbearance, and longsuffering, not knowing that the goodness of God leads you to repentance?

We must understand that God loves us even though we have sinned. To Jesus, we are not sinners saved by grace but rather we are His children and we have sinned and by His grace we are saved. My identity is not a sinner saved by grace; my identity is; I am a child of God. God made me into the image and likeness of my Father God and I know I am because Jesus says so. Jesus valued me enough to die on the cross for me. I have value and I am worth the pain that Jesus went through. And if I don't believe that, then the horrible death Jesus suffered was in vain.

If you cannot believe in the love Jesus has for each one of us, you are probably looking for your self-worth in the material things of this earth or in the approval of your friends. To transform hearts to God and to be His love to all; will be really hard for you. Please read on and let the Lord speak to you in the Scriptures He has chosen for this book. Please invite Jesus into your heart and accept the love of Jesus and Father God and come into agreement that Jesus can and will dwell in you. You must open your heart and mind to come into agreement Jesus is real.

John 1:29 The next day John saw Jesus coming toward him, and said, "Behold! The Lamb of God who takes away the <u>sin</u> of the world!

Notice the word sin is not plural. I believe the sin of the world John is talking about here is not believing in the love of Jesus and how special we are to Him. I believe not believing is the sin.

The revelation of how much God loves you is so powerful that it will take away all your past. I can hear your minds and in your minds you are asking, *"Who does this guy think he is? God will take away my past?"* I can tell you that I am a son of the most High God and I know for a fact I fall short of the mark! I no longer dwell on my shortcomings for I know if I dwell on them, I will only stay in them. I repent one time and by faith I tell Jesus, "Thank you Jesus for transforming me! Thank you for making all things new to me and thank you for forgiving me and right now I am available to you again; so let us do the work of the Kingdom." I choose to dwell on Jesus and He alone has made my shortcomings fewer and further between. Jesus alone has made my past a distant memory. Thank you Jesus, You are my favorite too and I believe you are real

Jesus came and died for our sin of unbelief. Jesus lived to show us He is real. Before I had a relationship with Jesus, I knew there were circumstances that would or could stop me from loving my Jenny or my children. Jenny and I had talked about what circumstances would cause us to split up. One was if either one of us had an affair on the other, our marriage was over. Our trust in each other would be broken and so would our marriage. I thank God that never happened!

Now, because of my love and trust in Jesus, I believe we could stay married even under those circumstances. Now, because of my relationship with my Jesus, I cannot think of a circumstance that would make me stop loving my wife and children. As human as I am, I do not believe anything could make me stop loving my children. The love of God is that perfect and God gives His perfect love to those who believe. I believe.

God is completely above all our circumstances. Jesus loved Judas knowing what Judas was about to do. If I knew you were going to turn me into the authorities and have me beaten and make me carry my own cross I, Ron Johnson the man, might not have been as forgiving as Jesus the man was at that moment. Now, because I walk together with Jesus 24/7, I believe I could forgive Judas like Jesus did. Everything is possible for those who walk with Jesus. I believe Judas killed himself not because Jesus could not forgive him, but because Judas did not forgive himself.

I believe I can be as courageous as Jesus. That probably sounds conceited doesn't it? But if you let Jesus love you, if you have surrendered to Jesus and truly have given your life to Him, then you will believe Him when He says *all things are possible!* Jesus the man was surrendered to His Father and look what my Father did with His Son. I am a son and my Father said He is no respecter of persons and I believe Him! DO YOU? Be a Son of God, saved by grace and loved by your Father God.

I believe Jesus was pure love and even when Judas was about to have Jesus crucified, the only thing that came out of Jesus was love. Jesus did not try to become love for all of us. Jesus is love for all of us. We all know we are made in the image and likeness of God. I believe the image and likeness Jesus showed us was the love of His Father God, Our Father.

Jesus never holds unforgiveness towards anyone and Jesus proves His forgiveness by living in forgiveness all His life. He never picked up any unloving spirit. Jesus never judged, Jesus had no bitterness, Jesus never had rights, but Jesus had favor with His Father and His Father cried out from heaven *this is my Son in whom I am well pleased!* Father has not done that for me yet, but I believe He will!

I know the Heavens will open someday and I will hear my Father say, "Ron you are my son in whom I am well pleased." That may sound arrogant but I say it is my goal. I am not just here to go to Heaven someday. I am here to bring Heaven to earth. I am here to give others Heaven on earth just as my brother, teacher, and best friend did! You see how easy that is? Just ask Jesus to make you into His perfect love and expect Him to do it! He will and I know it because I believe.

I can have the same relationship Jesus had with His Father. I know in Jesus all things are possible so I ask Jesus for the same close relationship that He had! I love my Jesus because He asks His Father for me to have the same relationship and our Father said yes. Thank you Jesus! I love you too! I live in relationship with my Father because I believe Jesus.

CHANCES THAT I MISSED

I'm still growing in this walk and here is an example of how much more I have to grow:

The other night around 9 P.M., I went to the campground's swimming pool and hot tub. I was there all by myself and talking to God while enjoying the hot water and bubbles. The gate opened and a woman walked in with her husband. She had a white gown on and you could tell she had a slender build. The way I was sitting she had to walk around the hot tub for me to notice her. She took her gown off and revealed a very little bikini. Her skin was so flabby; it covered or rolled over the little ties on the side of her bikini and her skin covered some of the bikini making it look smaller than it was.

I was sitting on the edge of the hot tub by the steps with just my feet in the water. She walked around to the handrail by me and bent over to hold on to the handrail as she went down the steps into the hot tub. I had closed my eyes as her bottom was right in my face as she entered the tub. Suddenly, the pungent smell of alcohol and cigarettes filled the air.

Her husband entered the tub and after they sat down in the water, I said *hi* to them. The woman started talking, which revealed her

31

smoking, drinking voice. I want to mention that as he entered the tub, he smelled of alcohol and cigarettes too, so I politely excused myself and walked the short distance to the table where my towel and shoes were.

I started putting on my shoes when I heard Jesus say, "I thought you wanted my eyes, my heart and my mind?" I said, "I do Lord, but I have a tough time talking to drunks especially when they put their almost bare bottom in my face." Jesus gently reminded me of what I had asked for from Him. I know I should have seen them as the children of God that He created. I should have risen above my own rule of not talking to drunks and seen them as Jesus sees them.

I just sat there at the table for a moment and listened to the two of them talking about some trashy movie they watched and thought was funny. Then after a short while, I got up and went to my camper. All the way to the camper, I was arguing with myself, saying I just don't talk to drunks. I just wouldn't turn around and go back to talk to them. I reasoned with myself, saying tomorrow when they are sober, I will talk to them. And guess what? I never saw them again.

Now I realized that Jesus had something for me to say to them and maybe it would have transformed their lives or at least I could have been a willing vessel for the love of God to flow through. But that night I actually argued with my Jesus.

I still have a lot to learn as you can see and I thank Jesus that He has forgiveness for me. I know in my heart that Jesus will not let that couple slip away and I know in my heart that Jesus will raise someone else up who is further along in his walk with Jesus than I am to talk to them. And that someone will get the Joy of the Lord that I passed up. I repented and moved on – and I know by faith that I am forgiven. Thank You Jesus, I love you too! Because I know Jesus loves me and forgives me, I can still grow and not beat myself up for that night. I thank God I am His son and I am saved by the grace of God because I repented. The best wisdom I know is that Jesus still loves me!

This is an example of how the love of Jesus cleans us up. About two years ago I was in a church and was asked to speak to the congregation there. After the service was over, a couple came up and asked me to pray for their daughter. They took me to the back of the church where she was sitting in a special chair. The only physical impairment that I noticed was that her eyes were not even – meaning they were not straight across from each other.

When our eyes met, she smiled as best she could and said that her birthday is in two weeks. I said, "I love birthdays!" and she replied that her birthday is in two weeks. Then, I asked her how old will she be and she replied again by saying her birthday is in two weeks. Her father gently put his hand on her shoulder and said "It's okay, honey, he knows." She immediately got quiet.

They looked at me longingly, they requested, "Will you pray for our daughter?" I felt prompted and asked, "What do you want me to pray for?" Then, they gave me a look, like *"Are you blind? I mean, isn't it obvious? She needs a healing!"* But I just stood there waiting for an answer. Then, the demeanor of both of their faces changed as the father of the girl spoke these words: "You want something specific to come against – come against the spirit of rejection!"

I asked, "Rejection? Why rejection?"

The father tells me, "Ten years ago when she was released from the emergency room and came home from the hospital after being involved in a car accident, her husband packed her stuff up and put her on our back porch, along with a note that read: I CAN'T DO THIS." He commented, "Her husband likes to play golf and it is a nice day today, so he is probably out playing golf right now!"

Immediately, I heard from my Jesus again and Jesus led me into this prayer, I asked "So you want me to pray for your son-in-law?" They looked at me with total disdain and said, "I'm sorry, but that is not what we asked you to pray for."

But my Jesus led the words as I prayed – for Jesus to make their son-in-law remember and to start honoring his marriage vows and the oath he freely gave to God and his wife in front of God and all his family and friends. In the prayer, I humbly said, "God, asked their son-in-law to remember how serious his marriage vows are and to come back into agreement with his vows." I ask God to open the eyes of the son-in-law to the joy of taking care of his wife and how this joy would supersede all the momentary happiness that any good golf score could ever bring.

As Jesus spoke directly to their hearts, I could sense their hearts transforming. I could not physically see their unforgiveness dripping on the floor or their rejection, or their hatred for their son-in-law but it seemed as though their sins were running down off them on to the floor! What I could see was the love of God flowing into them and I watched as God cleansed and replaced these sins with His perfect pure sweet love! Without even mentioning or any reference of the sins they were in, their sins were removed as far as the east is from the west! Oh, how my Jesus is the best!

Jesus transformed their hearts that day and their disdain for their son-in-law was removed forever. I remember walking to my car crying for joy as I had just witnessed the awesome cleansing power of God! And God never put any guilt or shame on them by saying you have a spirit of whatever and we need to war and cast it out so you can be free. The prayer never even mentioned any sin! Jesus simply freed them with His love and His Joy.

MAKE A DECISION

Asking Jesus into your heart is a decision that you need to make. Jesus and His cleaning crew will take care of the rest. The decision you make will last a lifetime when you decide to seek God with all your heart. Heavenly freedom from sin is just one decision away. My sheep know my voice, and our part is to listen. The pure love of Jesus is so powerful that it will remove your sin and allow His pure sweetness to cleanse us. Ask Jesus into your heart for freedom from the past, freedom from our burdens and freedom to look to a bright future filled with joy! The Joy of the Lord is ours by simply asking Jesus into our hearts. When you let Jesus into your heart you will see His transforming power change other people's hearts through you, one heart at a time!

Faith

I know by faith I am able to communicate with Jesus. Communicating with Jesus is the most important, the most fascinating and the most absolutely loving communication you will ever do. For us to transform the world one heart at a time we must believe in the power of God, we must believe by faith we are here to move mountains. For me, it would be really hard to have faith in anyone that I could not talk to. I believe Jesus knows how hard faith would be without communication, so Jesus opened the doors wide open and made Himself available for us 24/7. In fact, Jesus said to open our hearts and He will dwell in our heart 24/7. You simply must believe Jesus dwells in you.

Please don't ask me to explain how that works because I cannot explain how the Holy Spirit of God can live in each and every one of us. But I believe that His Holy Spirit lives inside of me and I know His Word is true. That is all I have to believe in – His Word and that is all I need. I believe and my reward is faith that can move mountains and I have His Word on that too!

To most people, the message 'transform the world, one heart at a time' is just too simple or even foolish to believe in. I believe in the Bible and Jesus said His message would confound the wise and the simple minded would understand it.

1 Corinthians 1:27 But God has chosen the foolish things of the world to put to shame the wise, and God has chosen the weak things of the world to put to shame the things which are mighty

The foolish thing God is talking about is His Message (transform the world one heart at a time; by faith you can have faith to move a mountain; and God's love is the most powerful force on the earth.) I believe that a lot of people think that the love

35

message is weak and you can and will be stepped on for living it. I believe the love message will confound the wise. I believe Jesus said someday every knee will bow to Him. The mighty do not understand this, but I believe Jesus lived the love message and proved the power in His love so we could live the love as Jesus did.

Romans 14:11 For it is written: "**As I live**, says the Lord, Every knee shall bow to Me, And every tongue shall confess to God."

Faith is knowing the goodness of God will leadeth thee to repentance. What is the goodness of God? There are many facets of God's goodness, but the one that encompasses them all is His love for us. We can lead the world to repentance by simply living the life Jesus modeled for us. Jesus said "as I live" and Jesus lived love.

It is not our goodness, neither is it not our love, but it is the goodness of God and the love of God that flows through us that will transform the hearts of others. I know that I could never carry my own cross all by myself, but with my Jesus, all things are possible! And when the time comes I will carry my own cross by keeping my focus on Jesus. For in Him, all things are possible. I actually love the idea of carrying my cross because it will shine light on what one man in right relationship with God can do. The love of God will confound the wise and confound the mighty, but through His love we will transform the world, one heart at a time!

Hebrews 11 is called the who's who of Faith. How do you recognize faith? Each one of these men went through tremendous trials in life. The trial brought out for a fact they had faith and believed in God. Under trial, their faith never wavered. Faith is the substance of believing in the perfect love of God. Please ask God for His mind, His eyes, and His heart and watch God perfect His mind, His eyes, and His heart in you. For when you have His heart, eyes, and mind you can live the life Jesus modeled for us. With these Godly traits in us, we will be able to withstand the trial and never waver.

For example, I don't believe the hate that came from Hitler was from Hitler, the man. The only place there could be that much hate is from the devil! Hitler became a willing vessel of the devil to let the hate of the devil flow through him. Do you know we are willing vessels of the devil every time we speak of any hate about anybody? Hitler is a darkening example of what one man filled with hate, or possessed with the devil can become! I think it is time to start discerning those thoughts we have in our head.

Jesus is the opposite of hate. Jesus is love! We can do more good by letting the love of Jesus flow through us and by being the love of Jesus to the world every day. Because with Jesus in us, we are more powerful than all of Hitler's military (the devil's military) combined. I really don't understand why the message of God's love is so hard for some people to understand. We see the devil's message of hate in the news going around the world every day. We see the result of the hate message is the need for militaries, governments, laws, prisons, and boundaries. The love of God is what sets us free from all the hate and its boundaries.

Jesus sees our potentials and not our sin! The night when those drunken bikini people came into the hot tub, I didn't see their potential. I looked at them with my physical eyes, my brain and my hardened heart. Jesus gently transforms me to see as He sees them as two lost souls, and to think as He thinks (the mind of Christ) and to soften my heart to love as He loves. See your potential and the potential of others by asking God to be your best friend. Ask God to be your teacher and your source of knowledge. Ask God to be with you everywhere you go and then believe Jesus is with you because He is! In my Bible, Jesus is called the Comforter.

John 14:26 But the Comforter, who is the Holy Spirit, whom the Father will send in My name, He will teach you all things, and bring to your remembrance all things that I said to you.

I know the apostles never thought they could be who they became until they met my Jesus. I don't believe we even have the slightest idea of our own potential until we meet Jesus and let Him transform our hearts into His heart. If you let Jesus transform your heart, you will find out what being made in the image of Jesus is all about. And all it takes is a little faith.

When you ask Jesus into your heart and start having a relationship with Him, He desires to be with you. The two of you will be talking every day and hearing every day. You will hear that still small voice of Jesus. Eventually, you will be ready to take on the world and transform the world, one heart at a time – by simply letting Jesus use your heart.

Become a willing vessel to let the love of Jesus flow through your heart. Then watch the world around you change and watch your heart transform other people's hearts, *one heart at a time*. Jesus proved it is possible and so I believe! Father God believed it was possible because He sent only One Person.

Thank you Jesus and Father God for loving me and transforming me with your love! Thank you Jesus for sending your Holy Spirit to comfort me, to teach me and to bring your words into my remembrance.

All it takes is a little faith.

Does Jesus Have Boundaries?

1 John 4:19 We love Him, because He first loved us.

This is probably the most misunderstood Scripture in the Bible. Eight little words with so much meaning because they take away the boundaries we have for ourselves. John says Jesus first loved us. How can we transform anyone if we don't have the love of Jesus in our heart? Knowing Jesus loved us first is extremely important and we must know Jesus loved us even while we were yet sinners and had boundaries and sin issues in our life.

The love Jesus has for us is so pure that nothing can chip away at it. I know today we are told to have boundaries. We are told to protect our heart. We are told to have prenuptial agreements. We are told to watch out for the little things that start chipping away at our love for each other. And the list goes on and on.

All these rules are man-made. Jesus gave us one rule, two commandments.

> **Matthew 22:37-39** Jesus said to him, "'You shall love the Lord your God with all your heart, with all your soul, and with all your mind.' This is the first and great commandment. And *the* second *is* like it: 'You shall love your neighbor as yourself.'

I don't hear any of those man-made rules in the Word of God, do you? I read the Scriptures again and I just cannot find anything about prenuptial agreements or boundaries! Once you give your heart to the Lord, you are protected. Notice that God said to love Him with *all* your heart. All means everything so don't hold back some to protect it.

There is nothing that can chip away the love Jesus has for you. In fact, it is His love for you that will enable you to live the life Jesus modeled for us so we can perform transformations boldly, just like Jesus did!

My love has no boundaries because my love is not my own, but the love of Jesus living in me. I gave Jesus all my heart. This is exactly why Jesus talked to me about my own shortcomings with the people from the hot tub. I made my own rule: *I don't talk to drunks because they never remember a word you say to them the next day.* I tell you, my rule is not found in the Bible. But my loving Jesus brought up this sin issue to me in love and I received His correction in love, so the love of Jesus grew in me. I didn't receive any guilt or condemnation, just His love.

Maybe, the couple in the hot tub could have remembered someone shared the love of Jesus with them. Perhaps I could have been that someone, that representative of the love of Jesus flowing to them. But instead I became a vessel of my own disdain for drunkenness. And I bet they remember my rejection even though they were drunk.

I love the gentleness of my Jesus and how He corrected me with His love. Jesus, I want your love flowing through me 24/7. I want your loving example to be my loving example. I want to be your loving example of forgiveness towards their drunkenness and I want to be your forgiveness to everyone and never again live by my Ron-made boundaries.

Maybe I could have been a mustard seed of love towards them and what God can do with a mustard seed of love is limitless because God has no boundaries. Maybe Jesus knew in my heart there was something that He wanted to gently remove from me through His perfect love. Thank you Jesus, I love you too! Please give Jesus all your heart and have all your heart protected so in your heart you will know there are no boundaries.

Later I was talking to my friend Joel, about the drunks I had encountered and he mentioned to me how sometimes when he is ministering to drunken people they get instantly sober. You see, my Ron-made rule that I should never talk to drunks etc. fails the test because Jesus doesn't live by any man-made rules. Thank you

Jesus for flowing your love and wisdom through Joel to me. I love you Jesus! Jesus has no boundaries and neither should I!

Life without Jesus is no life for me! Life without Jesus is living without any purpose. It is empty, it is void... Life without Jesus is not life at all. Life without Jesus is simply existing in this world until you die. Life without Jesus is a life of searching for happiness, but always being disappointed. Life without Jesus is a life of boundaries.

Life with Jesus is full of purpose – it is getting up every morning excited and asking God, "What are we going to do today." Life with Jesus is full of joy because there is no fear, no lack, and no disappointments. Life with Jesus is adventurous and fulfilling because there are no boundaries. Now that is my Jesus! Be set free! Be all you can be – live without any boundaries of hate, unforgiveness, and sin. If you know how much Jesus loves you, you would love ALL of Him too.

So how do we prove our love of God? Read in John and you will see how to prove your love of God.

> **1 John 4:20-21** If someone says, "I love God," and hates his brother, he is a liar; for he who does not love his brother whom he has seen, how can he love God whom he has not seen? And this commandment we have from Him: that he who loves God *must* love his brother also.

I believe my brother Jesus is talking about everyone being your brother. For example the couple in the hot tub. I'm sure I didn't see them as my brothers as I walked away. I hear people talk with hatred coming out of their heart for President Obama and didn't we just read that it is the goodness of God (in us His ambassadors) that will change a man's heart. Life is simple – just be the love of Jesus and watch ALL the world around you transform into a loving world we can ALL love and joyfully live in.

Jesus is also talking about seeing someone in need as our brother whosoever that may be. Just let the compassion of God flow through you. You will see amazing transformations in your brothers when you do!

I believe my Jesus wants us to prove our love of God! Our proof is in how we love one another. He that loveth God must prove it by loving his brother. 1 John 4:20 says *if someone says, "I love God," and hates his brother, he is a liar.* Those are some really strong words! I think it is safe to say Jesus does not want us to harbor any bad feelings towards anyone. Transforming someone while holding unforgiveness in your heart might seem impossible but letting the forgiveness of Jesus into your heart will make the impossible become possible! I love knowing that I walk in a world where nothing is impossible for me because I asked God to live in ALL of me. Jesus is perfecting me because I believe.

God makes everything clear that *if we love one another, God dwells in us and His love is perfected in us.* Yes, we have the Holy Spirit of Jesus and Father God in us ALL the time. When we start to understand by faith that the Holy Spirit of Jesus can live in us, we can believe Jesus is with us all the time. We prove through our actions what we believe; we prove His perfect love in us by how we let it flow through us. Faith is a substance and the substance of faith is us manifesting the perfect love of Jesus to everyone all the time.

I believe in 1 John 4:19, John is saying that if God didn't call us first we would not have His perfect love in us. Jesus could not expect us to manifest something that we don't have? You see, Jesus formed us out of the dust and there is no love in dust, so Jesus breathed His very own life into us, His very own image of love into us. In doing so, Jesus gave us the right to choose His love by walking with Jesus on His path of joy, love and strength or reject His love by walking our own path of becoming worthless dust again.

Dust without Jesus is a life without Joy, without strength and without His love. Believe me – without Jesus, we cannot transform hearts into His love because we cannot give away what we don't have! Remember that we are just dust without Jesus, without the breath of life in us we are worthless dust. Jesus had to love us first because having His perfect love in us would be impossible for dust.

42

To transform hearts we must know that we have the love of Jesus in us. We must know our source of love is Jesus. We must know and be rooted in the fact that we are worth the price Jesus paid (His own life). For Jesus is not a fool – He paid the price because we are worth it. Unlike earthly love, if you give physical love away you could run out because physical love is based on performance. The love of Jesus has no boundaries. His love is perfect! And just as Jesus corrected me about those drunken people, His love is still perfecting me. You see, Jesus loved me in my sin and just waited for the right time to correct me. Even the corrections of Jesus are love for He is love. Love is not what Jesus does, love is who Jesus is!

Have you ever met someone who has had their heart broken so many times they have just given up on ever being loved again? I know these people don't know Jesus on a personal level. I know these people are trying to get their identity from their relationship with another person and not their Creator, their Savior and the one who already laid down His life for us.

AN INVITATION

To the broken-hearted people of this world, I would like to invite you into a world of dying to self and living to be the love of Jesus to others. The broken-hearted usually have installed boundaries around their hearts to protect themselves from getting hurt again. Jesus asks us to die to ourselves. Your own protection system hasn't worked too well so far and it is actually removing you further from others and that is totally the wrong direction.

Jesus is asking you to trust Him and just let Him protect your heart. Ask Jesus to live in you and watch the love of Jesus fill the voids of pain and start you down a path of love, joy and strength again. You will wake up every morning, asking Jesus *"What are we going to do today?"* with a smile on your face and Joy in your heart. You will not need any protection system because Jesus Himself said He will never leave you or forsake you. That is a complete protection policy. When we simply ask Jesus into our heart we will live in the protection of knowing Jesus will never leave us or forsake us. Let your heart swim in the love of Jesus and you will overflow into the lives of others His joy, His peace, and His

43

strength to transform hearts into His love and that sure beats being broken and hiding and trying to protect ourselves.

Simply Let God Protect You

The campground I am in is hitting record-high temperatures so I have been going to the pool every day. With the air conditioning on high the camper still gets up in the 90's. This campground has an adult pool and a family pool. I go to the adult pool. Most of the people there are drinking alcohol and talking bad language. I ask Jesus on the way to the pool what He wanted to say to these people and I never got an answer so I didn't talk much to them.

The location of this campground is next to a dairy farm so the flies here are really bad. Sometimes, the pool will get covered with flies very fast! So when I am in the pool, I use a net to catch most of the dead flies on the water. Some people thank me and tell me I'm doing a good job. But there is one woman who asked me why I didn't let the people who are paid to clean the pool do their job. I told her that I like catching the flies in the pool because normally you swat flies to kill them and that only makes a mess. I said, "These flies are still fat and juicy and that makes them really tasty when you put chocolate on them." She didn't think I was funny.

One night, I went back to the pool around nine o'clock because the pool is open until 10 PM. There was only one couple in the pool and they were pretty drunk. They were part of the group that hangs out in the afternoon. I said, "Hi" as I went to a chair to take my shoes off. The lady asked me if I knew I was driving everyone at the pool nuts. I asked her, "How is that?" The lady replied, "They said no one can figure you out! You are always smiling and you even clean the pool with a smile."

She went on to say that some of the people there had seen me waxing my camper and they noticed that I was even smiling while I was waxing the camper. She asked me, "What makes you so happy all the time?" But before I could answer, her husband asked me are

45

you married? I replied, "Yes… Well kind of, I guess." He asked, "What does that mean?"

I told them my precious wife Jenny left me for a better man. But they were both pretty drunk so it took a couple seconds for my answer to register with them. He asked me, "Your wife ran off with some guy and you call this guy a better man? So I guess, you must have known this guy." I answered him, "Yes I know him. In fact, he is my best friend." Then the wife commented, "Isn't that always the way?" The husband said, "So that's the reason why you're so happy. You are divorced!" Then I replied, "Actually, I still consider us married." He quickly asked, "Wait! You called her precious after she left you for a better man?" I quickly replied, "Yes!" Then he asked me, "How do you know the guy she ran off with?"

I told them, "I consider him to be my best friend and I know she is a lot happier with him than when she was with me." Both of them looked dumbfounded and confused. Then the husband said, "Let me get this right: your wife runs off with your best friend and you are still happy about it?" I smiled and said "Yes!" Then he asked, "How long were you married?" I replied, "For forty years, six months, sixteen days and three hours!"

He told me, "You are weird." But I said "No. I'm not weird; I'm just peculiar because I am full of the Joy of the Lord." Then, they asked me, "How can you be full of joy?" I told them, "You see, within minutes of Jenny's passing I heard the voice of my Jesus say, 'Ron, Jenny is with me now'." The guy stopped and thought for a minute and said, "Oh! Your wife Jenny is in heaven!" His wife was laughing and said, "Now I get it! The better man is Jesus." Then I said "If your wife is going to leave you, it sure is comforting to know she left you for a better man."

I want you to know I miss my precious Jenny. I still consider us married because the vows we took said "until death do us part". Jesus came and destroyed death two thousand years ago, so I believe we are still married. You see I am not broken-hearted rather I am whole-hearted in love with my Jesus. I wake up every day with a purpose because I lay down my life for my Jesus with these simple words "Jesus, what are WE going to do today?" I believe Jesus gave me His heart because I asked.

46

Repentance

I met some adult missionaries a while back. They showed me some of their literature and it was impressive and very easy to understand. Their mission was to save souls by leading people into repentance and having them say the sinner's prayer. They had the Scriptures on handout cards to back up everything they taught. They had the backing from some churches to support them financially and they are very dedicated and even told me how many people got saved on their last mission trip. I am very privileged to meet them.

We are all part of the body of Jesus Christ and together we make such an important team for Jesus and His mission. I love to show people the love of Jesus and watch His love transform their hearts. Jesus in His word said it is His goodness that will lead a man to repentance.

Romans 2:4 Or do you despise the riches of His goodness, forbearance, and longsuffering, not knowing that the goodness of God leads you to repentance?

When my Jenny was still alive, I naturally tried not to hurt her in anyway because I love her very much. I never wanted to be source of frustration to her. Actually, I tried very hard to be a source of joy, love, and compassion to my Jenny. Because I loved Jenny so much, I would do things that brought her joy and showed her love and these works were easy for me. I had great joy in my heart when I saw her joyfully doing her chores as a mother and wife. I was very blessed with Jenny's love for me and together we are a team, because of the love that bonded us together.

I believe our relationship with Jesus is the same way. I believe if we are only taught to repent and come to Jesus sinful and sorrowfully, we are missing out on the best part of life in relationship with Him. Jenny never had to tell me to repent when I messed up. I realized I had hurt her and repentance was automatic. I would not go to sleep unless I had made a resolution to never hurt her again. Jenny usually didn't even have to point out my mistakes. I could tell by her attitude and I knew in my heart, because my heart would grieve.

I have a loving, walking, talking relationship with Jesus and although I have not even read the whole New Testament I know in my heart when I have grieved Jesus. I won't go to sleep; I don't want to breathe if I know I have done something to grieve my Jesus. My repentance is automatic and sincere and from my heart because I have the love of Jesus in me. And if even one drop of His love got replaced by my sin I will know it and I will change that bad behavior. I will change not because of fear of going to hell, but because I love my Jesus and I don't want to waste even one second of my life grieving Him.

My relationship with Jenny mirrors my relationship with Jesus. I make the needs of Jesus my first priority every day. I love waking up and having Coffee Time With Jesus and talking to Him every minute of every day. Jesus gave me a simple prayer years ago. Also, Jesus even made the prayer rhyme so I could remember it.

Dear Heavenly Father,

In Jesus name I pray, as I walk down the street today, I pray the people I see along the way, when they get home tonight and start to pray, will say "I think I saw Jesus today."

Jesus gave me this prayer April 23, 2011. I want to tell you my Jesus makes my life simple. I asked Him into my heart and I know Jesus is my heart. I asked Jesus for His eyes and I see as Jesus sees. I asked Jesus into my mind and I only want to think about what Jesus thinks about. Jesus in His word said that He made us in His image and likeness, anything else is less than He made us to be. Why would I want to be less then I can be?

Colossians 1:27 says, "Christ in you, the hope of glory". That is right! I have Christ in me and I Hope to be His Glory today. So I expect God to do great things through me today. I wonder how David in the Bible started his day.

I ask you, what did David use to kill the giant? I imagine most people would say David used a stone and a sling. When David killed the giant, he used faith in God. The stone and the sling were just the physical weapons he used. David spoke the victory before he ever went out to fight. David was not alone. David knew Jesus was real and with him. And his faith in God allowed Him to direct the stone to just the right spot.

> **1 Samuel 17:46-47** This day the Lord will deliver you into my hand, and I will strike you and take your head from you. And this day I will give the carcasses of the camp of the Philistines to the birds of the air and the wild beasts of the earth, that all the earth may know that there is a God in Israel. Then all this assembly shall know that the Lord does not save with sword and spear; **for the battle *is* the Lord's, and He will give you into our hands."**

Before the battle even started, David gave the credit to Our Lord. And I believe it was the faith of David that killed Goliath not a stone. Sometimes I wonder if David even aimed his stone or if he in his heart knew Jesus would send the stone where it needed to go. I have seen God do amazing miracles and I believe by faith that nothing is impossible. I want more than life itself to please God for I believe what Jesus said through Paul to the Hebrews:

> **Hebrews 11:6** But without faith it is impossible to please him: for he that cometh to God must believe that he is, and that he is a rewarder of them that diligently seek him.

Jesus said He is no respecter of men, so I know what He did for David He will do for anyone that will live in faith. Yes, faith in God moves the mountains and faith will transform your heart by simply letting God have His way in your life. Ask God for a revelation of His love for you individually and then watch God show His love to you unconditionally.

Four years ago, I asked God to let people see Jesus in me. I wanted my faith to shine like David's. I asked God to transform my heart and to let me be a vessel for His love to flow through to other people. And as a vessel of the love of Jesus, we can change one heart, at a time! Jesus knew what I wanted and Jesus knew what was needed to make that happen. Now, I am asking for a bigger revelation of the love God has for us. I know the most perfect love in existence is the perfect love that cast out fear. Perfect love is not our love for Jesus, but the knowledge that Jesus has His perfect love for us.

I know my prayers have changed. I no longer pray with an answer for God. Like I used to pray and tell God I need money for this and that. Now, I pray knowing God is the answer and has an answer so I don't try to figure out what the answer is or how this need will be taken care of. I pray knowing it is taken care of and I pray knowing God has an answer. I believe by faith that God has an answer and by faith, God is the answer. Simply let the love of Jesus into your heart and then let His love become a never ending river of His love to others. This perfect love will transform hearts, one at a time.

I know Jesus loves me perfectly. Do you know he loves you perfectly? I tell you this: to be a heart transformer you need to know Jesus loves you! You need to know Jesus is all knowing and Jesus knows your worth. Jesus did not pay too much for you – Jesus paid the ultimate price because you are worth the ultimate price the all-knowing God paid. Charity is giving and sacrificing. Charity is God's love for us and charity is how we love others.

When David got up that morning, his father told him to take some food to his brothers. Look what that simple act of obedience did and how it transformed the world forever. David was one man with a simple faith in my God, doing a simple act of obedience to his dad. You can have faith like the faith of David and with faith you can transform the world, if you just believe. Faith is allowing God to honor His Word through His love for us.

50

The River Never Runs Dry

In the Bible, the love of Jesus is likened to a river that never runs dry. Jesus said that out of your heart will flow rivers of living water.

John 7:38 He who believes in Me, as the Scripture has said, out of his heart will flow rivers of living water."

I believe in this Scripture, Jesus was talking about his transforming love. I believe Jesus equated His love to water to give us the picture of what each and every one of us can do if we just believe in God, the Father of love – Jesus came to earth to show us! Pastor Dan says love is not what Jesus did. Love is what Jesus is. Become love and become Christ-like.

Matthew 5:45 That you may be sons of your Father in heaven; for He makes His sun rise on the evil and on the good, and sends rain on the just and on the unjust.

Water is needed for life. Water is what we clean everything with and water rains down on the just and the unjust alike. So water doesn't discriminate against anybody. I believe Jesus used water to describe His love because Jesus in His Word said the rain will fall on the just and the unjust. The love of Jesus doesn't discriminate. The love of Jesus is available for those who answer the call to follow and those who don't. I believe the river of life described in the Bible is likened to a river of the love of Jesus.

How do we become a river of life? Jesus made His requirement very clear: *He who believes on me.* We are to believe on Jesus and we know the Father because we have seen Jesus, we can hear His voice, and we can become rivers of His endless love by simply believing. People will know Jesus is real when they see Jesus in you! Please be an ambassador of Jesus and transform a heart today by simply asking Jesus into your life. Listen for His voice. Know you are a CHILD of God and be available!

Do you see why I believe water is likened to the love of Jesus? Water will clean the just and the unjust. Water will satisfy the thirst of the just and the unjust. When we flush the dirty water down a drain, where does the dirt go? When Jesus cleans you up where does your sin go? I believe the Love of God is even more merciful and more available than water. This is my crude way of making a comparison but there is no real way to make a comparison of anything to the love of God! Please accept Jesus into your heart and you will have joy beyond your understanding.

JUDGMENT AND GRAY AREAS.

Matthew 7:1-2 Judge not, that you be not judged. For with what judgment you judge, you will be judged; and with the measure you use, it will be measured back to you.

Life seems pretty simple to me. I often hear people talk about gray areas and how that makes everything so complicated. I know Jesus has no gray areas for He says you are either for me or against me. So in order to become the perfect love of Jesus, we must believe God is able to transform us into the perfect love of Jesus! We must believe His love is capable and is within us. We must prove our belief by how we love others around us. (Not judging others) Please, let the love of God flow through you today! You will see the results in the eyes of others. Jesus said the eyes are the windows to the soul.

Let's talk about gray areas for just a minute or two. Have you noticed how in all of man's laws, there are gray areas? For example, the speed limit is 60 mph and everyone knows you can go 65 mph and not get a ticket. This gray area might even allow you to go to 70 mph with some police officers, but you might run into one that will give you a ticket for going 61 in a 60. To venture into the gray area is up to you and whether or not you get a ticket is totally up to the officer.

There were a lot of gray areas in the Old Testament. And today, people are still arguing over these gray areas. All of their reasoning and all of their studying leads them to think they are right and someone else is wrong. Jesus never argued to convert someone. Read in John 8 how Jesus the man transformed the heart.

John 8:4-5 They said to Him, "Teacher, this woman was caught in adultery, in the very act. Now Moses, in the law, commanded us that such should be stoned. But what do You say?"

See how they reasoned from the law and self-righteousness, being puffed up by their knowledge. Read on and notice Jesus never argued or debated. The life of Jesus was and is an example of love at work and an example for us to live by.

John 8:6-9 This they said, testing Him, that they might have *something* of which to accuse Him. But Jesus stooped down and wrote on the ground with *His* finger, as though He did not hear. So when they continued asking Him, He raised Himself up and said to them, "He who is without sin among you, let him throw a stone at her first." And again He stooped down and wrote on the ground. Then those who heard it, being convicted by *their* conscience, went out one by one, beginning with the oldest *even* to the last. And Jesus was left alone, and the woman standing in the midst.

I believe this proves that their hearts were for being convicted by the love of Jesus. If not, they would have stayed and argued.

John 8:10-11 When Jesus had raised Himself up and saw no one but the woman, He said to her, "Woman, where are those accusers of yours? Has no one condemned you?" She said, "No one, Lord." And Jesus said to her, "Neither do I condemn you; go and sin no more."

The love flowing through Jesus convicts, but never condemns. The love of Jesus set the captives free. Some people think when Jesus said go and sin no more, He was saying to her; do not live in adultery anymore. I believe people living in adultery are looking for love. Jesus through His forgiveness gave her a big dose of true love and asks her to believe she is loved by Jesus. "Go and sin no more" I believe Jesus was saying go and unbelief no more. She received forgiveness (love) not unforgiveness (hate), she received conviction not condemnation, she received life not death and she received a lighted narrow path, not the darkness of sin. She received pure sweet forgiving love of God, not the fear of judgment and the stoning of the law.

John 8:12 Then Jesus spoke to them again, saying, "I am the light of the world. He who follows Me shall not walk in darkness, but have the light of life."

I believe the girl received the Light of life and I believe we are here to be the Light of life just as our teacher Jesus was. It is simple. Just ask Jesus into your heart and listen for His voice. We are His ambassadors and Jesus gives us His words of love.

With Jesus, there are no gray areas or maybes. The girl was set free! Removing gray areas is simple for Jesus. For example: Jesus said if you harbor hard feelings or hatred towards your brother, you have committed murder in your heart. There is no gray area there! You are committing murder in your heart. Jesus said so a man thinks in his heart so is he. Jesus said you will stand in judgment for murder. Please guard what you allow into your heart and please allow God to please himself by you simply listening for His voice and allowing Jesus to consume your heart. Be the light of life! Be forgiveness to all. Be a believer and a follower of Jesus.

To some people, grace is taught as the gray area of God's Word. But I don't believe in that at all. Simply put, grace is the love of God to have mercy on us. God's love allows us time to turn away from our old ways and follow in the way of the Lord. For me, man's laws have gray areas because men can decide or make a judgment call whether to break the law or not. This gives the person judging power in himself. Please don't look for earthly power in yourself but seek ye first a relationship with Jesus and Father God and come too know their supernatural power you have inside you to transform a heart into the love of Jesus.

Jesus said we are not to judge for Jesus is our only judge. If we choose to judge we will be judged by the standard of our judgment. These are not my words, but His.

Luke 6:36-37 Therefore be merciful, just as your Father also is merciful. Judge not, and you shall not be judged. Condemn not, and you shall not be condemned. Forgive, and you will be forgiven.

The good news is with Jesus we have grace and because of grace we are given time to repent and be welcomed back into His loving embrace so we may be the children of our Father in heaven. Jesus through grace removes the sin as far as the east is from the west. The love of Jesus is truly the best.

You see, there are no gray areas with Jesus but there is total removal of sin. And unlike the record keeping of man's laws 'this is the third speeding ticket so you are going to jail' we have forgiveness of sin with Jesus and removal from the punishment of sin, if we are smart enough to take advantage of God's grace, God's love is for all "the just and the unjust" please repent and believe we are forgiven.

Let your light shine on the evil and on the good, send your love to the just and the unjust for if we as children of God start judging others we will be judged according to the standard by which we judge. I believe Jesus gives us time to seek Him. I believe Jesus made us ambassadors for us to shine His light (His Love) in the darkness of this world. When we shine His love, other people will see it, and we can transform other people, one heart at a time! We are to be ambassadors without fear. For we know Jesus is always with us and always here.

Remember that repentance is a gift from God that comes right into your heart and that repentance in your heart is what sets you free from the bondage of sin. Remember that Jesus paid the price so we are free to do the work of the kingdom and do as Jesus did: set other captives free. Let Jesus transform your heart and then transform hearts today by setting them free just like Jesus did.

There are no gray areas in our life. We are either captives in bondage or free in the love of Jesus to be the love of Jesus to others! I choose to repent and God set me free. I choose to listen to God and God talks to me. I choose to accept His love and God made me His son. I choose to be transformed from the one who needs ministry *(weak, broken and depressed)* to the one giving ministry *(full of light, life, love, Joy and strength)*. Jesus first loved me and Jesus first chose me and now I choose to be an ambassador of the love for Jesus by simply fearlessly following Jesus. And I follow by simply reading His Word and as I read I listen for His voice. I read His word not for knowledge to argue or to impress others with my knowledge but I read His word to be transformed into the love of Jesus. Jesus is my love and my transformer. Jesus is the one in whom I will trust and never worry.

Please read Coffee Time With Jesus in the Joy of the Lord book. If you don't have one call and I will send you one free. 513 377 1727

The Next Step Is Listening

So how do you get to know God and have such a personal relationship? The answer is by listening!

My good friend Joel once showed me a DVD about a woman living in Africa. This woman neither could read nor write anything in any language. But amazingly, this woman can quote the Bible and transform hearts for God because she hears from God and has great discernment about who she is listening to! Her life is a walking testimony of God's love and what one heart in loving communication with God and living with God's Holy Spirit inside you can be! She is a living testimony of what God can do with a willing vessel.

Spending quality time with Jesus is actually listening for His voice. I know those of us who can read need to have Bible time. I know in our personal life there are plenty of jobs that need to be done and there are a lot of distractions. But our priority must be to listen for the voice of God.

John 10:27 My sheep hear my voice, and I know them, and they follow me

Please read all of John 10 and you will plainly see that Jesus tells us to listen for His voice. To discern His voice is the most important discernment you will ever have.

Matthew 6:33 But seek first the kingdom of God and His righteousness, and all these things shall be added to you.

I believe to seek first the Kingdom of God is to listen for His voice. I know there are people who will tell me that I am wrong.

To *seek ye first the kingdom of God* is to read and study His Bible. Studying the Bible will give you head knowledge. Jesus said head knowledge puffs you up. Yes, read your Bible about the life of Jesus, but not just to know of His life and be able to quote it. Read to become as close to Father God as Jesus was. Read the Bible so you can do all that Jesus did. Read to become so close to God that you can discern His voice over the voice of a stranger. Believing is becoming and becoming is Faith and faith is knowing Jesus honored His Word, whether you see it or not.

Discerning His voice will form us into God's righteousness – that is right standing with God and then, all these things shall be added unto you. The last part of this Scripture has been quoted a lot. If you read all of Mathew 6, you will see what the 'all these things shall be added unto you' this Scripture is not talking about material possessions which is sometimes taught.

Mat 6:33 But seek first the kingdom of God and His righteousness, and all these things shall be added to you.

The gifts John and Matthew are talking about are bringing Heaven to Earth in your heart. You want the gifts? Just become John 10 and become Matthew 6 and you will become Christ-like. And being Christ-like is the gift from God. It is living in Heaven right now. The truth is in the Scriptures. You will transform the world as Jesus and the Apostles did *'one heart at a time'*.

When I talk about listening, I do not mean to listen for specific instructions every day. For example, I never heard God say, "Ron, go to Wal-Mart and find someone wearing pink gloves with a green tennis racket and no shoes to pray for."

The listening I hear brings me into a close relationship with Jesus. I never try to make things happen. I just ask God "What are we going to do today?" and something just happens.

For example, the other day while visiting friends, we were talking about Jesus telling us to come to Him as a child. I told them that I think Jesus was talking about not having an agenda. A child doesn't get up with all this pressure to perform and get something done. A child of God simply asks God, "What are we going to do today?"

You see, I have no bricks and no mortar so I have no boundaries. I am a believer of Jesus Christ so I am free to be where He wants me to be. I simply listen for His voice as I go about this day – His day, the day He has given me. Today is a day to be thankful for. Today is a gift from God so use it wisely!

Luke 9:48 And (Jesus) said to them, "Whoever receives this little child in My name receives Me; and whoever receives Me receives Him who sent Me. For he who is least among you all will be great.

I come to my Jesus as a child of God. I believe Jesus can mold us and make us into His image a lot easier if we come to Him as His child. I have become a child in my faith and I will be a child because I believe the truth of my Jesus without reservations. A child learns early on to discern the voice of His parents. I will simply listen and trust in God.

Here is a story about trusting, listing, believing, and never tempting; even if the temptation to lie seems harmless.

The other day, I met a 5-year old little boy named Billy in the campground. This boy Billy comes from a broken marriage. He was together with his dad and his dad's girlfriend and they seemed very happy. I was on my way to the campground pool when I met them and so they asked if I would take Billy because he loves to play in the water. I said, "Sure!" On the way to the pool, Billy asked me my name. He started calling me Uncle Ron. We had a great time playing in the water and I could tell we were connecting. Billy's dad came and got him a couple hours later.

The next couple days we became really good friends. I had dinner with them and had time to share the love of Jesus. Billy's dad and girlfriend seemed to view me more as a babysitter than a friend, but that was okay with me. Billy and I talked every day. His childlike faith was on display all the time. The fourth day, another little boy named Jimmy came to visit Billy. I learned they were friends from their neighbor back home. Soon, I became Jimmy's friend also and we all spent time together, because it seemed that every day Billy's dad and his girlfriend had some place to go.

The three of us – Billy, Jimmy and I went to the pool. While we were there one day, I saw Jimmy hide Billy's shoes. He told me that he was playing a game and asked me not to tell Billy where his shoes were.

When we were about to leave the pool, Billy started looking for his shoes. He asked Jimmy and Jimmy told him that he doesn't know where they are. Then, Billy asked me if I knew where his shoes are and I said, "I'm not sure." Then, Jimmy told Billy where his shoes were and said "Uncle Ron saw me hide your shoes!"

Immediately upon hearing this, Billy got so mad and upset. He walked over to me and screamed at me, "You're a liar, I hate you! You are a liar! I hate you, I hate you, I hate you!" I picked Billy up and we put our foreheads together. I looked right into his piercing brown eyes and said, "I'm sorry, Billy." Billy let me hold him and we continued staring each other eye to eye for maybe an hour as I explained to him how sorry I was and I continued begging forgiveness.

Finally after an hour or so, Billy did forgive me. And I will never forget his piercing eyes as he stared into my eyes like he was looking for a devil in me. Later in my Coffee Time With Jesus, Jesus spoke to me about trust. Jesus in His Word said, "He will tempt no man." Jesus reminded me of a story we shared in the Joy of the Lord book about trust. I had totally blown Billy's trust in me, all for a stupid joke. Jesus asked if I noticed Billy was not mad at Jimmy, because their trust was broken a long time ago. Billy could not trust his dad, his mother, his dad's girlfriend, etc., but Billy thought he could trust me. Please read FRUITS in the Joy of the Lord book. If you don't have the book call and I will send you one free. 513 377 1727

My heart was broken for I knew I had betrayed Billy's trust for a stupid joke. We became friends again and enjoyed each other's company. But I could tell our relationship was a little different. If they didn't have to go back home at the end of the week I would still be there for him. I believe the love of Jesus will mend the hurt in Billy's heart and mind. When it was time for them to leave, Billy hugged me so tight and I hugged him back, as if I could adopt him. I learned a very valuable lesson and I pray for Billy every day. I thank God for His love and for His corrections and I thank God for mending Billy's heart and mind.

Discernment is so important. Focus on Jesus is so important. Learning who we are listening to is so important. Please focus on Jesus like Jesus asks us to do and never break someone's trust for a stupid joke. I will listen... I will listen and by the grace of my precious Jesus I will be transformed. Thank you Jesus I love you too.

LISTENING TO GOD

The other day I was asked to go on a bike ride with some friends, named Gary and Paula. I thought, "I haven't been on a bike for over twelve years." But still, I gladly accepted and they had an extra bike for me to use and so off we went. We rode down to the Pacific Beach. While riding down the boardwalk I saw two severely handicapped and mentally challenged teenagers in wheel chairs. Their parents were pushing their children on the board walk. As I went by on my bike, one of the children looked up and as our eyes met, she smiled and lit up like a Christmas tree. She even tried to talk, but just made a verbal noise. My heart wept inside for them, but I just kept going.

Gary was out in front of us somewhere and Paula stayed with me so I would not get lost. Paula saw the girl light up like a Christmas tree so she paddled her bike up alongside me. Paula asked if I wanted to go back and pray for them. I said, "Yes, I do. But I need to talk to God first. I didn't want my prayer to make them more aware of their children's situation. I believe our prayers should be prayers of the compassion of Jesus. Not sympathy of the world and not guilt, shame or condemnation, by warring against a devil or telling them they must have sinned or their parents' sins was carried forward, as is taught in some denominations."

We continued down the boardwalk. I prayed and heard from God. In about 20 minutes we arrived at our destination, where we met up with Gary again. Gary wanted us all to have breakfast and said he would go ahead of us because there is always a long line at the restaurant. As Gary left, Paula asked me if I had heard from God. I told her, "Yes, Jesus gave me some Scriptures for the parents. Paula wanted to hurry back to pray for the children, but I said that there's no need to hurry for they will still be there. I knew in my heart that God wanted me to talk to them so I don't need to hurry. I knew Jesus had a plan and Jesus would make it happen.

We went back and sure enough the children were still there. I asked the parents if I could pray for their children. The mother answered yes almost reluctantly. I started by asking if they knew the Scripture where the apostles asked Jesus about the man who was blind from birth. They replied, "Yes, we know that story." So I continued to tell them that the apostles asked Jesus who sinned, this man or his parents? At this point the parents got a look on their faces like 'here we go again, we must of sinned or our children would not be like this'.

I asked the parents if they remembered what Jesus told the apostles. They said that they couldn't remember. I told them, "Jesus answered the apostles, saying that neither the parents sinned, nor did the child sin, this one is for the glory of God."

I said, "I believe your children are here to manifest the glory of God and they will manifest the glory of God just like the blind man in the Scripture did. I believe God never makes a mistake and His work is always perfect, so I know your children a mistake. I believe we believers are called by faith to call healing into existence. So today, I call for the manifested glory of God to be present with your children because I know all things are possible for me by calling on the name of Jesus Christ my Savior. Jesus in His Word tells us He is no respecter of persons so what He did for the blind man He will do for your children."

The parents had a look of disbelief on there face, so I said, "You don't have to believe or even have faith. The faith has to be in the one asking not the one receiving, after all you are not asking for anything. I don't believe the blind man or his parents had any faith to see their son's sight restored that day. I don't believe they got up that morning and said, 'Jesus the man, who is a Son of God will come by today and restore our son's sight."

I continued, "Jesus was a man who knew He was a Son of God and God the Father honored the faith of His Son and healed the blind man. God the Father is my Father and that makes me His Son. I believe my Father is going to heal your children today."

I added, "It is plain to see in the Scriptures that Lazarus had no faith to come back from the dead, but Jesus the man asks his Father and again our Father honored the faith of Jesus the man."

The mother almost cried and thanked me for the prayer. She then asked me, "Where did you learn to pray like this?"

I told her, "I don't know how to pray like this, these are not my words. When I passed by a little while ago, your daughter lit up like a Christmas tree." The mother said, "Oh yes, I saw that."

I continued, "I didn't stop to pray right then because I felt a prompting in my heart not to rush and Jesus prompted me to talk to Him first. I started asking God what He wanted to say to you. These are not my words. God gave me these words for you and your children."

The mother looked surprised and said, "God wanted to say these things to me?" I said, "Yes, He did." She said "God wants to manifest His glory in my children" I said yes He does.

The parents were overwhelmed by God's love so I thanked them for the privilege to let me pray for their children and I hugged both children, then I continued on the bike ride.

Paula, who was watching from a short distance, asked me if I was disappointed because nothing seemed to happen to the children. I said, "No. I do not need to see the miracle to know it happened." I will stand in faith the rest of my life that the children are healed today. I have prayed and stood in faith before and then found out years later that the day after I prayed the miracle happened. Seeing the miracle does not change my faith, my faith is in my God, not in watching miracles.

My identity is in my God, whether the miracle happens in front of me or not – it doesn't change the fact Jesus is real and lives inside of me and I know the miracle happened. If God wants me to know, He will bring the awareness of the miracle to me. I simply believe like a child that I am a child of God and I believe Jesus loves me. I know and I believe that I saw a miracle of hope in the parents that day and I believe I will hear someday about their two children coming out of those wheel chairs and the miracle will also bring glory to my Father because they are perfectly healed. Thank you Jesus! I love you too.

Then we went on to breakfast. As we were eating, Paula asked why I was quiet. I said, "I was just thinking about what God had done this morning and it is only 9:30 in the morning. What will God do this afternoon?"

The Scripture story Jesus gave me that morning is John 9:1-7:

John 9:1-7 Now as Jesus passed by, He saw a man who was blind from birth. And His disciples asked Him, saying, "Rabbi, who

sinned, this man or his parents, that he was born
answered, "Neither this man nor his parents sinne
works of God should be revealed in him. I must work the
Him who sent Me while it is day; the night is coming when no one
can work. As long as I am in the world, I am the light of the world."
When He had said these things, He spat on the ground and made
clay with the saliva; and He anointed the eyes of the blind man with
the clay. And He said to him, "Go, wash in the pool of Siloam"
(which is translated, Sent). So he went and washed, and came back
seeing.

I love my Jesus, but greater revelation than this is knowing no
one can love me more than Jesus. The great love of my Jesus will
shine through to other people, only if we asked Him to let us
become His vessel of His love to other people. Because nothing is
impossible for Jesus! His perfect love will change other people.
Please listen to His voice, asked Him every morning, "*Jesus, what are
we going to do today?*" And you will be amazed on how Jesus will
touch other people's lives through you. Truly life in Jesus is
amazing

Foolishness

Jesus talks about foolishness in His Word. I cannot speak for other countries, but here in the United States, I believe foolishness is very much alive. Especially in the U.S. television, radio and internet – these are full of foolishness. Today, we think of foolishness as entertaining and we make foolishness a lifestyle. Foolishness fills up time where we don't have to think. I remember watching Gilligan's Island on television when I was young. The show was so simple-minded that you did not have to think! You just sit back, relax and watch it. A relaxed mind is a great place for the devil to wreak havoc.

To me, it seems like there was a turning point in television. I mean, up to a certain point in our history, television shows had morals – we had serious dramas and true-life stories etc. and never plain foolishness. Now, from what I hear about the shows on television today, they display what the world I grew up in would have called *bad morals*. Bad morals are accepted now because they are presented through foolishness and humor.

The television show producers have learned that foolishness and humor relaxes us to the point they can slip in their bad morals and life changing beliefs right into our living room. Either we don't notice it or we choose to ignore it. Or sometimes we think the problem is just too big so we don't even try to change it. Like everything that is bad, a bad agenda starts by slipping in just a little bad and then they spoon-fed us Christians their poison until we become desensitized.

For example; the Barney cartoon show for children started with a seemingly harmless song I sang with my grandson every morning. (I love you do you love me?) Seems harmless and yet Jesus showed us love is Charity, giving and sacrificing. Most divorces come about because one spouse didn't GET what he or she wanted out of the marriage. I remember the words to a very popular song years ago; "when you just give love and you never get love, you better let love depart." We are inundated with these thoughts from everywhere. I remember telling dirty jokes thinking I was funny and really I was grieving the Holy Spirit with my mouth. I believe we need to ask God for discernment because we are letting foolishness into our homes and our hearts by not discerning our thoughts. Foolishness is going to Google for answers when you do not know who Google's source is. Simply put Jesus needs to be our source. Let us look at where God put foolishness in His book:

> **Mark 7:20-23** And He said, "What comes out of a man, that defiles a man. For from within, out of the heart of men, proceed evil thoughts, adulteries, fornications, murders, thefts, covetousness, wickedness, deceit, lewdness, an evil eye, blasphemy, pride, foolishness. All these evil things come from within and defile a man."

I believe all these sins mentioned in Mark have found their way into our living rooms through the television and we became totally desensitized. I believe that foolishness is the catalyst or entry-point for the rest of these sins. Notice Jesus tells us the origin of sin is the heart. For all these sins come from the heart and defile the man.

> **1 Peter 5:2** Shepherd the flock of God which is among you, serving as overseers, not by compulsion but willingly, not for dishonest gain but eagerly

I think the devil read 1 Peter 5:2 and is doing it really well together with his willing accomplices – the television and radio show producers and the internet. The devil is the master of twisting the Scriptures and using them against us. The devil is feeding the flock with foolishness by making it look harmless.

I am so joyful I have Jesus as my personal best friend. I have His answer in my heart and a personal instruction book called the Bible. I live as Jesus did. I transform one heart at a time and we –

Jesus and I win. I am so blessed that Jesus showed me how even just a tiny bit of foolishness (Uncle Ron where are my shoes?) changed Billy's trust in me, but not forever because of the love and forgiveness of God in Billy, we are set free to love each other again

Jesus puts foolishness right up there with some really big sins of the heart. Our part is to recognize the foolishness of the worldly programming on television, radio, internet, etc. The answer is so simple to me. We need to ask God for discernment and stay focused on God. Then we will stay away from these sources of foolishness and TURN THEM OFF. Jesus tells us to guard our minds. Jesus also tells us to guard our hearts, and Jesus says to have a watchman at the gate. Please people, respond to my Jesus. The answer is not complicated! Let Jesus transform your heart and you will be ready to transform the heart of the person next to you because there is someone they can transform next to them. This is how God works! Learn how to discern His voice and listen to Him. Through this, we can change other people's hearts, one at a time!

Please don't give foolishness a place in your heart. For if you do, you are spending your time getting to know the one you will spend eternity with and it is not Jesus. Foolishness is deceitful and will take away your mind from Jesus. Foolishness robs us of our morals by making morals foolish. Jesus calls foolishness a sin and so it is.

I choose to not be foolish. I choose not to look at the sources of foolishness. I choose to follow my Jesus and my reward is a path of joy, strength and peace beyond understanding. Jesus makes me a free flowing river of love to everyone I meet. This flowing love will eventually change other hearts, and these changed hearts for Jesus will transform other people too!

You will not find a relationship with Jesus on the internet, television or radio because Jesus is not there. Why are you spending time there? Simply ask Jesus for His heart, His mind and His eyes. Jesus loves me and this I know because Jesus wakes me up every morning to tell me so. I love you Jesus and I choose to follow YOU and not the foolishness of the world! Thank you Jesus for walking, talking and being with me everyday. I love your joy and I love how you wake me up everyday.

68

Bible Study

Today I was talking to my Jesus and Jesus reminded me of a Bible study I went to a couple years ago. The man running the Bible study had a series of DVD's for the men to listen. I happened to be there for the first teaching of the series. The teacher on the DVD said, "As you watch this, you will need to have your remote in your hand because I will ask questions." He wanted the leader of the group to pause the DVD and let the group who are watching answer the questions to each other.

The leader asks, "Can anyone here give us an example of something God has done through you this week?" No one put up their hand except me. I gave them an example of what God had done this week. Then they resumed the DVD and the teacher asked if anyone had a written testimony from anyone that would declare you to be a Christian? Again, no one raised their hand except me. The leader of this group looked at me in disbelief and asked, "You have a written testimony from somebody?" I said, "Yes. I keep them in a folder in my car. I'll go get the folder if you would like me to."

The leader said, "Alright, we will wait. You can go and get the folder." I brought in the folder and handed it to the leader. The leader started reading the testimonies. And then with watery eyes, he asked me, which one do you want me to share with this group Ron?" I said, "Just pick one."

After he read one testimony to the group, some of the men in the group looked astonished. I looked at them and said, "All you need to do is let the love of Jesus flow through you to others. To do that, just ask Jesus into your heart and listen for His voice. When you pray, don't just go to God with a list of wants and needs and then run on your way saying I have to get to work or I have to pick the children up, etc. Please listen for the voice of Jesus. This is the most important thing you will ever learn. You will hear Jesus call you by name and your heart will jump for joy!"

No one likes to talk to someone who is not listening. Not listening to God is why people backslide in churches. In church we are taught to do for God. We are taught if you do this for God; God will love you. That is so wrong. We can spend our entire life working for God and still be like servants – not having a relationship with our God. We cannot be good enough to earn God's love, for God's love is a gift; but we can please God by our faith! By faith we hear from God. By faith we are to become one with God and we are to recognize His voice. We are the ambassadors of Jesus and as such we are made Sons not servants. Servants never know the love of their master, but WE DO. We are the sons of God who serve.

Jesus in His Word tells us He wants us to hear and to recognize His voice. To recognize the voice of God, we need faith that we are hearing the voice of God. I believe by faith all things are possible; so by faith, I hear the voice of God. Jesus is not some distant person off in heaven somewhere. My Jesus is right here in my heart. He likes being here. Jesus made me. Jesus likes to spend time with me, Jesus calls me by name and I talk to Jesus all day long. I have a special time set aside every morning and every afternoon to have Coffee Time With Jesus. Jesus is in my bedroom every morning and Jesus wipes the sleep out of my eyes every morning as He wakes me up. I don't wake up trying to please Jesus. I know by faith, I am pleasing Jesus and Jesus tells me how much He loves me!

Every morning I ask my Jesus, 'What are we going to do today?' I don't want to get dressed without Jesus. I don't want to breathe or speak a word, or eat anything without thinking about my Jesus first. Jesus is my source of life, knowledge, wisdom, understanding and most of all love. I truly cannot be the love of Jesus without Jesus in me. Jesus opens doors for me all day long. I know for a fact that if I am going the wrong way Jesus will turn me around.

Please make the decision to make Jesus first in your life. After all, Jesus invited us to follow Him. I think it would be hard to follow someone who is second in your life. Making Jesus first in your life will let Jesus give you the gift of trust. You will need to trust Him. I cannot even think of a day where all my trust is not in God. Trusting will become love. Love will bring us into a communion with God that is intimate. You will receive an everlasting understanding of His love for you. Jesus will call you by name just because He loves you and you are His creation, his masterpiece, you are the one He came and died for. Believe Jesus loves you and receive His love.

When our goal is to transform hearts, we want to see results. We want everyone we meet to experience Jesus and to experience His love. I sometimes get so excited that I forget to slow down and see His goodness. Jesus has so many blessings if we go into the fast lane and try to please Him by what we do, we will definitely miss a lot Jesus has for us because we are leading not following.

I believe sometimes Jesus just wants to hold us so near to him and he wants us to experience His personal touch and most of all take time to hear His voice. When Jesus asks me to have Coffee Time with Him, I remember I cried and I ask Jesus, "You mean *you* want to have coffee with me?" Jesus replied, "Yes, we need to talk every day." Jesus wants to talk to you every day and Jesus wants you to take time to listen also.

I remember a while back when I had the privilege to talk and spend the day with a group of young married couples in Columbus, OH. At the end of our time together, the men gathered around me and asked, "Ron, we know you were married forty years and so we want to know what you think is the best way to keep your marriage together?" I told them that a great marriage will mirror a great relationship with God.

We can have a great marriage and a great relationship with God by simply listening! No one likes to talk to someone who is not listening. If you stop hearing your spouse, eventually she will withdraw. If your priorities are elsewhere, your spouse will notice and she will be hurt. I believe our relationship to Jesus requires us to set time aside every day to hear from Him also. One of the most important lessons in the Bible is what I call 'dying to self'. Truthfully, dying to self is living for others – Jesus, your wife, your children and others. Simply set time to listen to Jesus and to your spouse and you will have a great marriage.

What Is Truth?

Jesus said, *"I am the way, the truth, and the life. No man cometh unto the Father but by me."* Wow! I am so in love with my Jesus! I mean can any other person on earth claim to be all of these: *the way, the truth and the life?* Can any other person even claim to be one of these? No one can! A friend of mine named Pastor Dan said, "Jesus said, 'I am the way, the truth, and the life'. Notice it doesn't say 'I am *a* way, *a* truth, and *a* life'." JESUS IS <u>THE</u> WAY, <u>THE</u> TRUTH AND <u>THE</u> LIFE! Jesus is not a way, a truth, and a life. There is only one way, one truth, and one life and Jesus is all these three.

Whenever I hear people say they seek the truth, I cringe. Because I know the only way they have to judge truth is by what they know physically. If they haven't invited Jesus into their hearts yet, these people who are seeking truth are missing the way, the truth and the life. Their search for truth will leave them double-minded and unstable in all their ways and always in need of more information. They will remain that way until they meet a true representative of Jesus who will show them Jesus and be able to talk to them about seeking God who is the truth.

Jesus proclaimed Himself to be the truth and I believe Jesus. Jesus proves the truth by who He is, what He does, and the fruits of His life. I don't need any scientific experiments or scientific laws or scientific findings to point me to the truth! The truth of Jesus comes through our faith manifesting His truth every day. The truth of Jesus is the manifested healings, His manifested love and His manifested life we live in everyday.

Some of us Christians try to be His love and try to show people His way, and maybe even try to bring His life to others. Our problem in most cases is we are <u>trying</u> to put Jesus on like clothes. We dress up and try to do something nice for someone.

Becoming Christ-like isn't dressing up for an hour a week and praying in church and then watching to see if your prayer worked. The truth of Jesus has to be established in our heart. I know a man who prayed for over a thousand people before he saw one person healed. He had the truth of Jesus established in his heart and would not stop praying for people because the truth didn't seem to work. Now almost everyone he prays for is healed.

Becoming Christ-like is living the life of Jesus by being the life of Jesus 24/7. Jesus is love so you must become love. Following Jesus is simply allowing Jesus to have control of your time. Heaven on Earth, the Joy of the Lord, the strength of God is yours and mine by a simple YES LORD. Simply agree to be a vessel of HIS LOVE, HIS LIFE AND DIE TO YOUR SELF.

Jesus tells us that He is the truth and He cannot lie. Jesus also tells us He is love so we know from the Scripture Jesus is truth, light, life and charity and the greatest of these is charity. Charity is giving your life to others and dying to yourself. We saw this truth in Jesus and we will see this truth in all believers of Jesus Christ.

The Love of God will purify your heart. God's love flowing through you will transform hearts – from cold and indifferent to becoming the hot love of Jesus. You cannot see love until love becomes an action. So there is a spirit of love called Jesus. And by inviting His spirit into your heart you can manifest the spirit of love physically. When you invite Jesus into your heart, you are inviting the spirit of light, love, life, hope, faith and truth into your heart.

You will watch Jesus gently transform you away from the worldly or fleshly desires of momentary happiness into pure heavenly desires of transforming hearts into His love one at a time.

Jesus will delight your heart with His heavenly love and you will recognize the spirit of Jesus because with Jesus, you will receive true spiritual joy and strength. It is the joy of Jesus in your heart that people will see physically. The Joy of Jesus in your heart will attract them to the Jesus in you.

You will become the light to the path to Jesus. And by being the light of Jesus, you will become a vessel for the love of Jesus to transform hearts into a life of charity and living for Jesus! To be a vessel for Jesus, all you need to do is dedicate your life to Him by making yourself available to Jesus. Just wake up and ask Jesus, "What are we going to do today?"

You will never ever be discouraged. Discouragement is from the devil. Paul's writings remind us our works are of faith, our labors are of love and patience is our hope in our Lord Jesus Christ. Sometimes, it seems that no one notices our loving forgiveness or our acts of kindness. Sometimes, no one seems to care. But we who are of Christ know that these actions are not made to be noticed here on Earth, but we are noticed in the sight of our loving Father God. If you want others to notice you, compliment you or build you up, etc, you are trying to receive your self-worth from others instead of what God thinks about you. This is the perfect recipe for failure. Being a child of God is knowing that you are a son of the most High God. Jesus loves me and that is all I need to know. Self-esteem is an earthly show that I don't need to know.

1 Thessalonians 1:3 Rremembering without ceasing your work of faith, labor of love, and patience of hope in our Lord Jesus Christ in the sight of our God and Father

Although the devil has filled the Earth with momentary happiness, there is nothing on Earth that will bring the true joy of Jesus like a true relationship with Him and by letting Jesus transform your mind into the giving and sacrificing charity of Jesus. The transformation I am talking about is not you saying 'I love you Jesus!' The transformation I am talking about here is revelation heart awakening knowledge of how much Jesus loves you!

I pray for Jesus to wake my heart, to open the flood gates and let the love of Jesus, your love Jesus flow through me and be on Earth as it is in Heaven. Thank you Jesus for being in me and now let US (Jesus and I) transform a heart today. Jesus, thank you for putting Your Spirit upon me, in me and through me. I love you too! Heaven on earth is not a dream; it is being a vessel of God's love to all we have seen.

You are truly transformed when you know that Jesus loves you! Like Jesus said, "I am the way, the truth, and the life!" Jesus went home to be with His Father in Heaven, but before He went, Jesus gave us the gift and privilege to be His ambassadors here on Earth. Please use your privileges. Read about the life of my Jesus in His book and you will see Jesus passed the responsibility of every heart on earth to us His ambassadors. Yes you and I have been given the privilege to be ambassadors for Jesus. As ambassadors of Jesus, we can transform this world, one heart at a time!

Luke 4:18 The Spirit of the Lord is upon Me, because He has anointed Me to preach the gospel to the poor; He has sent Me to heal the brokenhearted, to proclaim liberty to the captives and recovery of sight to the blind, to set at liberty those who are oppressed;

Jesus covered all of us in Luke 4:18 and every affliction known to man; so go preach the gospel to every nation and if you have to use words. Preach knowing the Spirit of the Lord is upon you. Preach knowing you have the truth living inside you. Preach boldly knowing you have the best teacher in this world and live to be a vessel of the love of God. Transform a heart today and see a real new world order.

What Is Trust?

In our world today, we are taught not to trust anyone. Rich people are told to have a premarital agreement. They will be viewed as stupid if they don't have one. You see they are already preparing for the worst. In the event of a divorce, the rich person won't have to give up or share their wealth. My question is this, *what is trust?* You see, we have redefined trust into *don't be stupid and lose everything you worked for.* The person you love might be a fraud and their only aim is to take away your wealth. Yes, that is trust – trust in yourself, your trust is in your lawyer, your trust is in court systems, your trust is in everything but God. Jesus said we are to put our trust in God.

You see, if your trust is in God you will hear from Him every day and you won't need to ask him if the person is right for you to marry because you will recognize the love of Jesus coming out of the person and you will see His love in their eyes. You will trust because you will recognize the love of Jesus in them, for His love defines them. There is only one true love. Jesus is love and He wrote the book of love. Read His story in the Bible and how in the New Testament, Jesus came to show us the love of our Father. You will not be deceived ever when you put your trust in Jesus because your faith is in the one who cannot lie or leave you so in Him you can trust!

Today we are told to have insurance for everything. We have insurance for our health, our belongings, and our land. If you could step away from your life long enough to see how crazy that is – how much effort we spend to just pay the premiums, I am sure we would see how absurd our trust in insurance must look to Jesus. I mean, we know we cannot take it with us and in our heart we know we never really own it. Yet, we will wear out ourselves, trying to keep it. Really, everything is a gift from God because life is from

God and without life what do you need any of that stuff for. Please put your trust in the giver of life.

Along with trust comes rest. When you trust in God you will rest in God. The opposite is true also! If you have your trust in yourself, you have no rest. I hear people say they cannot sleep. They have no rest and are tired all the time. To me the answer is so simple, if you cannot rest, you are not trusting God. Rest comes from trust in God and trust comes from faith in God and faith comes from belief in God and belief gives us hope in God. Put all that together and you have the Joy beyond your understanding Jesus talked about. Joy gives you strength and with strength you will know all things are possible and that takes you back to trust in God and knowing Jesus loves you is the peace that gives you rest.

So what is trust? Godly trust knows if someone wrongs you today you can trust in God for I know for a fact I am okay because Jesus is in love with me and no one can take His love away. My love and my hope and my trust are in the one who said, *"I will never leave you nor forsake you."* Thank You Jesus! I love you too!

Here is an example of trust. Please read how Jesus called the apostles, He simply said, "Come, follow me." Think about that for a moment. James and John were in the boat with their father, mending their nets. They were busy because they were getting ready to go fishing. They must have heard of Jesus. They had enough knowledge to know they were interested in hearing more about this man called Jesus. Do you see the sequence of being called? They knew of Jesus and they had heard of Jesus. So when Jesus called them to follow, they did. This is trust.

The results of the apostles trusting Jesus are explained in the Scriptures and we are all reaping the benefits of their trusting Jesus. If we also choose to trust Jesus and trust in God, our life becomes so simple. Because we will know Jesus is at the helm, He is in our boat or walking on water to come save us. Follow Jesus and live in the kingdom of God now.

Matthew 4:17-22 From that time Jesus began to preach and to say, "Repent, for the kingdom of heaven is at hand. And Jesus, walking by the Sea of Galilee, saw two brothers, Simon called Peter, and Andrew his brother, casting a net into the sea; for they were fishermen. Then He said to them, "Follow Me, and I will make you fishers of men." They immediately left their nets and followed Him. Going on from there, He saw two other brothers, James the son of Zebedee, and John his brother, in the boat with Zebedee their father, mending their nets. He called them, and immediately they left the boat and their father, and followed Him.

Jesus is calling us today. Jesus still gives us the same option to follow Him. In the bible we are told for a rich man to lay down all that he has worked for can be very hard to do. It seems easier for a poor man to answer the call to follow Jesus because he has less to lie down, but I believe that is a judgment call of man. I believe we are all called and when we lay down whatever we have to follow Jesus, the result of our following Jesus today will be as great as the apostles we read about in the Bible.

Rich or poor, you are called to a new realm of trusting by faith in someone that you have never seen. Someone you have just read about and someone who you hope to hear from. To follow Jesus is to allow Jesus to transform your life into a life of hearing his voice and by faith alone following the voice of Jesus. Life will become so simple when we discern the voice of Jesus.

Today, just like in the days of the apostles, we are called to be followers of Jesus and we are to be examples of Jesus. Jesus said you will recognize His followers by their fruit. Just as the apostles bore good fruit or transformations, so will we who follow Jesus to become examples of Jesus. Jesus gave believers the tools to transforming lives; the tools are the power to raise the dead, to heal the sick, and to cast out devils with the words of Jesus. We believers have the actions of Jesus and the love of Jesus flowing through us. We have all this by trusting and believing and faith in my Jesus.

Please notice the difference between tools and fruits. We believers are to use the tools, healing, casting out devils and raising the dead to help others believe. A fruit is a transformation of a non believer into a believer. Fruits are not the healing, not the raising, and not the casting out of devils. The healing, the raising and the casting out of devils are tools to set people free from the bondage of unbelief. Tools help non believers accept Jesus is real and to accept Jesus into their heart. The transformation of a non believer into a believer of Jesus is the fruit and the reason Jesus came.

We see in the life of Jesus how Jesus the man used these tools by faith in His Father in heaven to give or bring heaven to earth. By faith, we are like Jesus. We have a big tool box when we let the transforming love of Jesus transform us into a believer and allow Jesus into our hearts so we too, by faith have access to all the tools.

I don't want just a healing ministry, I don't want just a deliverance ministry, and I don't want to be known just as someone who just raises people from the dead. I want people to see Jesus in me and His joy to shine through me. I want the love of Jesus to flow into the hearts of others and transform their hearts. I simply want Jesus in my heart and to allow Jesus to transform lives of others through His love in me. The rest of His blessings are automatic. Jesus gave me all the tools because I believe.

You might be asking what I mean by *automatic*.

I have Jesus in my heart so I have healing to give to others. I have deliverance to give to others and I have life in my heart to give to others. I can give life whether the others are alive or dead. Jesus is in my heart so all things are possible (automatic) for Jesus to do through me. Follow Jesus into an amazing life of love and transforming hearts one at a time by simply believing.

Jesus gave us the power to perform miracles and Jesus says don't get excited about that. Then Jesus tells us why we should rejoice! Jesus said to us, "Rejoice because your names are written in heaven!" Thank You Jesus that my name is written in your book. Thank you for telling me that no one can pluck me out of your hand. The only way I can lose my salvation is for me to give it away by not discerning my thoughts. (Listening to the devil).

Fearlessly trust in Jesus. Jesus protects us on our journey. Jesus tells us, "Nothing by any means will hurt you." Remember nothing means nothing. I tell you this, the devil cannot hurt you! Jesus calls the devil a nothing! Jesus protects you so trust in Jesus and be fearless.

Luke 10:17 Then the seventy returned with joy, saying, "Lord, even the demons are subject to us in Your name." And He said to them,

"I saw Satan fall like lightning from heaven. Behold, I give you the authority to trample on serpents and scorpions, and over all the power of the enemy, and **nothing shall by any means hurt you**. Nevertheless do not rejoice in this, that the spirits are subject to you, but rather rejoice because your names are written in heaven."

For just for a moment or two, please let me try to describe the ministry of Jesus. Jesus had no boundaries. He has no limits, no fears and no needs. Jesus operated in all the gifts of the Holy Spirit. Jesus proved that nothing is impossible for you, when you live in relationship with our Father. Jesus transformed the hearts of everyone who listened and ask Him into their heart.

Jesus had the greatest ministry the world has ever seen and he didn't even have his own bed to sleep in. Jesus had no bricks and mortar and no place of His own. Jesus even allowed Himself to be hung naked on the cross, so Jesus left this world without any earthly possessions.

Yet, Father God performed so many miracles through Jesus. The Bible says, "If you tried to record them, the world could not contain the books." Jesus was called teacher, master etc. but the title above them all was Son of God. Calling Himself the Son of God got Him killed. Being the Son of God, he rose from the dead and proved that He had all life – this life and the next in His hands and the devil (nothing) could not touch it.

I believe we are to declare we are a Son of God to the world and we have a ministry of calling believers into the love of Jesus to transform the world one heart at a time. I believe all the power of Jesus has been given to us if we will only believe. In your walk with the Lord, please do not call on the name of Jesus to see if it works. Only call on the name of Jesus because you know you are loved by Jesus and you know He is your brother and because you know there is nothing Jesus will not do for you. The love will flow, the tools will work and lives and hearts will be transformed!

Jesus the man told the apostles:

John 5:19 Then Jesus answered and said to them, "Most assuredly, I say to you, the Son can do **nothing of Himself**, but what He sees the Father do; for whatever He does, the Son also does in like manner.

The Son can do nothing of himself. Isn't that amazing? Jesus admits that He can do nothing on His own. But in relationship with Our Father, the Son can do all things and did all things. This is Jesus telling the apostles, "I in myself can do nothing of myself." Then Jesus tells us who His power source is. For what He seeth the Father do is what Jesus does.

We have the same Father. We have the privilege of sharing in the Sonship of the Father. Yes, we can be Sons of the most high Father God and walk in the privilege of being a son by simply believing. The Father gave His only Son at that time. I believe Jesus told us to focus on God and Only God because all these things will be added when we do. I believe Jesus and so I know there is nothing my Jesus and I cannot do! Be a believer and be a transformer.

John 14:10 Do you not believe that I am in the Father, and the Father in Me? The words that I speak to you I do not speak on My own authority; but the Father who dwells in Me does the works.

Here we see the requirements: we are to believe we are in the Father and the Father is in me, here is the reward for believing 'the words I speak unto you I speak not of myself'. Yes, Father God will give us the words to transform hearts to Him. Jesus also tells us we don't do the work, (I cannot heal anyone by my self) the work is performed by the Father through us when we choose to have the Father dwell in us. Choose to let our Father dwell in you in the form of the Holy Spirit and Father God will give you the words and He will do the works or miracles through you, like He did through Jesus. We are to be vessels of His transforming love. All this is possible because Jesus told us so and I believe Jesus.

Please don't try to please God by your works. We just read Jesus could do nothing of Himself. I see so many people burn there self out trying to please God. I have actually heard people say if God would just give me the money I could do all these great things for Him. Jesus was simply obedient to His Father. Jesus is our example; Jesus only did what He saw His Father do. Jesus never needed anything (money) to build His ministry. Think about when Jesus told the apostles to feed the multitudes and the apostles checked to see how much money was in their purse. They did not have enough money to feed everyone. Money never stopped Jesus and money should never stop you from doing the things we see Jesus do. Your works have to line up with what your Father needs to be done not what you think needs done. Simply become a vessel for God to flow through you by allowing Father God and Jesus and the Holy Spirit to dwell in you and then listen for His voice. When we become like Jesus we will become God's vessel of His love, we can transform this world, and change other people hearts so they too will become God's loving vessel for other people.

Please never try to make something happen on your own. Simply let the love of Jesus flow through you by inviting Jesus into you. Your heart will never be the same. You will touch lives in ways you never dreamed and your walk will be fearless. Follow the Master, follow Jesus and the world shall be reconciled to my Father. And on judgment day you will hear how pleased Our Father God and Jesus are to see you did their will on earth and Father God and Jesus will welcome you home. I am anxiously awaiting their welcome home but I am joyfully spending my days here because I know I am a Son of God and I know I can help bring the kingdom of God to everyone I meet.

Contradictions in Scriptures?

What seem to be contradictions in the Scriptures can rob us of faith unless we go to our source: Jesus. Ask Jesus to explain these contradictions to us. When you are out in the world, transforming hearts to Jesus, you may run into people who will try to trick you with what appears to be contradictions in Scripture. But Jesus tells us we need not worry because Jesus is with you and He will protect you. Here is a sample contradiction I encountered:

1 John 4:12 <u>**No one has seen God at any time**</u>. If we love one another, God abides in us, and His love has been perfected in us.

John 14:6-7 Jesus said to him, "I am the way, the truth, and the life. No one comes to the Father except through Me. "If you had known Me, you would have known My Father also; and <u>**from now on you know Him and have seen Him.**</u>"

Jesus Himself says that no one has ever seen His Father. Then Jesus says you seen me you have also seen the Father. Doesn't that sound like a contradiction in Scripture? How do we transform hearts to God when the Scriptures seem to contradict their selves? We go right to our source, and simply ask Jesus our teacher for an answer.

Jesus was his Father's ambassador while He was here on Earth. Now we are the ambassadors for Jesus. I tell you this: there are no contradictions in the Scriptures at all. Jesus has told us we are to be ambassadors for Him and as ambassadors we represent Jesus to everyone just like He represented His father to us: *"You see me, you have seen the father."* As ambassadors for Jesus, when people see us they should see Jesus. When people see us as being ambassadors of Jesus, they should see the way, the truth, and the

83

life of Jesus! Some would say Jesus is figuratively speaking. Jesus was an ambassador for His Father. We are the ambassadors for Jesus, so people should see Jesus in us literally.

When I still had my woodworking business I used to listen to radio a lot. After listening for a while, I had developed a mental image of the person speaking. This image was based totally on the morals and the voice as I listened to the person speaking on the radio. I was totally surprised when I saw a picture of him physically! Yes, after listening to him for years I thought I already knew what he would look like and what his responses would be. I believe our relationship to Jesus is like that.

We know what His response is going to be. We recognize His voice, but we have no idea what Jesus and the Father look like. I believe they made our relationship this way so we would hone our listening skills as well as our discerning skills to such sharpness so we cannot be deceived. You see, we are able to recognize Jesus in others by their morals and what their responses are to life circumstances. Also, we will hear the morals of Jesus in others and recognize them as followers of Christ no matter what they look like.

In John 14:6-7, I believe Jesus is making a distinction between seeing physically and hearing physically versus seeing and hearing spiritually. Sometimes, it would appear as though the Scripture contradicts itself until you check the contents in which it is written by going to Jesus your source. In order for us to have seen Jesus, Jesus had to become a physical person – He had to lay down all His Godliness and became man.

Jesus became man to show us our Father is a Father of love and understanding – full of compassion to the point He sent His only Son to show us Himself. Jesus said, "*You see me, you have seen my Father.*" When we order our life after the perfect example of Jesus we too are becoming pleasing to our Father God whom we know through our Brother Jesus Christ.

Now we see there are no contradictions in the Scriptures at all and if ever someone asks you about what seems to be a contradiction in Scripture you can rest knowing Jesus will explain them to you. You can rest knowing Jesus will help you to transform the heart of the one in front of you because Jesus is using you to reach out and show them His love for them!

Like our Teacher Jesus, we are to transform the hearts spiritually by using the Words of Jesus from the Scriptures we read physically and yet the Words of Jesus become spiritual words of love as we speak them for all to hear! We also are to model the life of Jesus physically because we are the ambassadors of Jesus here on Earth now.

Yes, we are His representatives physically and can represent Jesus physically through our actions and speech. We hear from Jesus in our spiritual hearing all day long, and we can read about His physical life from the Bible. When we model our lives after Jesus and tune our ears to Jesus, spiritually we can become His representative here on Earth. And we will change the world physically one life at a time, and spiritually we will transform one heart at a time.

JESUS NEVER ARGUES

About a year or so ago, I was talking to a man that I met in the campground. He was obviously very well-versed in the Bible. He quoted the Scriptures and had way more Bible knowledge than I. After talking for an hour or so he asked me if I knew the meaning of a certain Bible passage? He read the passage to me. I told him that I didn't know the meaning of the passage. He looked a little puffed up and said, "I thought you would know the meaning of this passage. You claim to be an ambassador for Jesus, don't you?"

I read the passage twice and still couldn't figure out what God was saying in them. Then the man said, "So, did I stump you?" I told him that when I don't know the meaning of a Scripture I just go right to my source, Jesus. Then I ask Jesus out loud, "Jesus, what are you telling us in these scriptures?" Then we both sat quietly for a minute and after a while, he asked me sarcastically, "Well, what did Jesus tell you?" I told him that I didn't hear anything. Again, he sarcastically asked me, "So now, what do you when your teacher is quiet and doesn't answer you?"

I answered him, "Obviously, the answer is not important for me to know right now." His looked at me with total disbelief and

85

asked me, "So you are telling me that your Jesus didn't answer you because these Scriptures are not important to you?" I answered him, "No. Like I said, the answer is not important to me *right now* or Jesus would have told me right at this moment." He seemed turned off by my answer and shortly later he left my camper.

As soon as he left, I went to my source again and ask Jesus, "What happened? Why didn't you tell me the answer right away, just then Jesus answered me, "All the man wanted to do was argue." I said, "Jesus, we never argue, do we?" And Jesus said, "No."

I totally rest in the love of my Jesus to take care of me in any circumstances. I rest because I know I am loved by Jesus! Can you imagine the freedom in knowing Jesus loves you? Freedom is knowing that Jesus first loved me and now I follow Jesus by simply loving Jesus, who is in me. Jesus commanded us to love ourselves and now because I love myself as a child of God, God can love others through me. I simply love Jesus who loves me!

Simply model your life on the Way, the Truth and the Life of Jesus and you will transform hearts just as Jesus did one heart at a time. Now that's faith in my Jesus! Jesus in His Word said, "Without faith it is impossible to please Him." Yes, you can please Jesus by faith and your faith will please Jesus but His love for us will never change and by faith I know I am His favorite! Calling me His favorite is not arrogance. It is my goal.

The devil has his counterfeits of these spiritual gifts for you. For example: happiness versus joyfulness or charity versus love, and sympathy versus compassion. The answers to these questions are in the Joy of the Lord book. If you do not have one call me and I will send you one free. 513 377 1727

In your relationship with Jesus, ask Jesus for discernment and you will easily recognize the devil's counterfeits of hat verses God's love etc. By seeking Jesus and by seeking to be the life of Jesus here on earth we will become the ambassador we are called to be.

I Have Never Seen Jesus, Have You?

1 John 4:12 No one has seen God at any time. If we love one another, God abides in us, and His love has been perfected in us.

The Scripture is very clear: "no man hath seen God at any time." While on Earth, how do we know something is real? The usual answer is we go by our senses – we cannot touch God, feel God, see God, smell God or taste God because with God we are called to a higher system of belief.

Let's say your friend just bought a new car. They pull the car up in front of you and you can see the new car, feel the new car, touch the new car, and smell the new car etc. and through our senses we believe there is a new car there! That seems simple and you don't even need faith to believe there is a new car there. The problem comes when our senses are all we believe in. We know there are some people that make a living deceiving our senses. We call it magic. Magic is the art of deceiving our senses. We know our senses can be deceived, yet most of the time we rely on our senses to make decisions.

What is the higher system of belief we need to trust in to know God is real? We need FAITH! Faith is a higher system of belief. By faith, I hear God... By faith, I feel the presence of God... By faith, I walk with God... By faith I am protected by God! By faith in the Grace of God, I know my record of wrongs has been removed and forgiven. And I can be set free by simply repenting, asking God for forgiveness, and by faith I know I am forgiven.

In John 4:12 we see how to be perfected: *"if we love one another, God abides in us and His love is perfected in us."*

I want more than anything on earth to be perfected by Jesus. I will simply love everyone the way Jesus did because Jesus dwells in me and I will be perfected by Jesus. Jesus said, "No man hath seen God at any time." We are the ambassadors for Jesus so if someone wants to see God they need to look no further than you or I! Yes! You and I have the power to show people Jesus! God is so awesome! God has faith in you and I to be His ambassadors.

Listen for the voice of God right now and transform the heart of others right now. Do one heart today and see five million hearts in thirty days.

Do you need to see God to know He is real? I haven't actually seen God but I know He is real. The only requirement to know God is real is faith.

John 20:29 Jesus said to him, "Thomas, because you have seen Me, you have believed. Blessed are those who have not seen and yet have believed."

I tell everyone I'm blessed and I truly am! I'm blessed because I have Jesus in my heart and I'm blessed because I know by faith He is real. I'm blessed to know Jesus will use you and I. When Jesus sees our faith is real; Jesus will make the impossible possible for us. And we know by faith in Jesus, we can transform the world one heart at a time because all things are possible.

Truly Transformed Lives

It was March 15ᵗʰ 2014, and I'm sitting here in my camper and talking to my Best Friend Jesus and I remember my precious Jenny was still here with me last year on this date. Then, I started thinking about when Jenny died and how some people thought I would be mad at Jesus. People thought I would even lose my faith and maybe even tell God where to go. I guess my faith seemed shallow to them.

I believe Jesus is in the transforming business. I believe Jesus is in the *'setting us free'* business. I believe Jesus is in restoring relationships. I believe Jesus is transforming us through His love for us. The transformation I am talking about here is not, "Hey, say the sinners prayer and get saved forever," "it is not about getting a bus ticket to heaven," and "it is not once saved always saved."

The transformation I am talking about will last forever. It is a transformation that will endure and will bring true change in your desires. God will align your desires with the desires of God. This alignment will bring true peace, true Joy and true perfect love. And through this you will be able to transform others by what they see in you.

For me, the Joy of the Lord is planted deep in my heart. When life puts pressure on me – like when my Jenny died, I am blessed with a relationship with my Jesus that will see me through my trial. I live a whole new lifestyle. I am being transformed by Jesus every day. I know Jesus loves me! That seems so easy to say but if you truly know Jesus loves you, you will pick up your cross and follow Him and become an ambassador of love.

I know when Jesus was here on earth He was just a man, He could not have done the things he did without knowing His father loved Him. My Father's love had to be planted deep in Jesus the man. I know this because if every one of your best friends deserted you when you needed them the most, most of us would be broken. Jesus carried His cross all the way to my Father's feet and then laid it down with more forgiveness than the world has ever seen.

I want to be the Jesus faith ambassador. I want to be the Jesus love, and I want to be the Jesus forgiveness! I want forgiveness that is so perfect; I can put the trespasses against me away as far as the east is from the west. I have Jesus living inside of me so nothing is impossible for me! Thank you Jesus!

HOW JESUS TRANSFORMS LIVES

Here's an example of how Jesus transforms lives. They proved to me that He is real and alive today and will flow through YOU only if you just give Him permission to. This story happened a few years back, and this is the most requested testimony I have from people who have heard it. I believe it shows us that when you know you have Jesus inside of you, all things are possible and you will not live in fear.

Jenny and I were living in our motor home and we had been on the road for a very long time. It was late in the afternoon when I asked Jesus to find me a campground. I told Him I was tired and I just wanted to get off the road. I said to Him, Jenny and I have been in the camper for two days and so I ask Him for a campground with black top roads because I wanted to get Jenny out of the camper and take her for a walk in the wheel chair. It was a beautiful sunny day and I could tell the wind was picking up because it was blowing the camper around a little. I thought this weather is perfect to walk in and to have Jenny outside.

The next road sign I saw had a picture of a camper on it and so I knew the next exit had a campground. I took the exit and followed the signs to the campground. I was totally blessed and excited to see the campground had black top roads. I thought, "Jesus, You really do look out for Jenny and I!" I love you Jesus! So I went into the office and paid for the night.

This campground was shaped like a mushroom. It only had a little bit of road frontage but right past the office it opened into a big area. The stem of the mushroom is where the overnight people would stay, up front by the access road. So after I paid for the night, I made a U-turn and pulled into an overnight spot. From where we were parked I could see the office.

As I was leveling and hooking up my camper, the wind speed picked up even more, you could smell the rain and hear the thunder. Lighting started crackling and the smell of the rain became stronger and the force of the wind intensified. I went into the camper and looking out of the windshield. I put my hand toward the windshield and said, "In the name of Jesus, I command this rain storm to stay out of this campground until I am done walking my Jenny".

I walked to the car to get Jenny's wheel chair out. I brought the wheelchair alongside our camper; I carried my Jenny out of the camper and tied her into the wheel chair. There were a couple of people in the camper next to me who were eating their dinner. He opened his window and asked me, "What on earth are you doing?" I said, "I am going to take my Jenny for a walk." He replied, "Are you nuts? Can't you see and smell the rain? Can't you hear the thunder roaring and see the lightning crackling?" I told him, "Jesus gives us the power over the weather so I have commanded the rain to stay out of this campground until I have walked my Jenny." He replied with, "Oh, one of those Jesus freaks," and shut his window.

After tying my Jenny into her wheelchair, we then started down the road towards the office and the back of the campground. As we approached the office, I could smell the faint smell of a cigar. Even in the strong wind and with the rain not far away, I could smell the cigar. As we drew closer to the office, I could see a man sitting in a chair on the large covered porch. He was the one smoking the cigar I smelled.

Jenny and I were on the road in front of the office when I hollered over to him "I love the faint smell of a cigar." He looked at me and said, "I don't give a damn whether anyone likes the smell of my cigar or not. I'm going to smoke it!" I told him, "Wow that is a fine attitude. Is everything okay?"

His answer surprised me.

He went on to tell me how he had been diagnosed with cancer two years ago and at that time he was given only five years to live. He continued, "So I only have three years left to live and I'm wearing coveralls because I have a colostomy. If I want to smoke a cigar, I will. And I don't give a damn whether you like the smell of it or not."

"Do you know Jesus?" I asked. Looking annoyed, he replied, "Oh, just what I need. Another person to tell me about Jesus." He then asked, "And what in the world are you doing out here anyway? Can't you see it is going to rain hard any second?" He looked at my Jenny and asked, "Is that your wife in the wheelchair? He continued the two of you are going to get drenched any second now, so I suggest you should get her back to your camper as fast as you can."

I beamed, "Yes, this is my wife. And yes, I do see all the signs of rain coming! You see, I believe in Jesus and so before I left the camper I commanded the rain to stay out of this campground until I'm done walking my Jenny." He told me, "You are crazy! It's blowing! You could hear the thunder and lightning striking. You can even smell the rain and I can already feel the mist of the rain." He repeated again, " you better get to your camper now!"

He added, "And you know what? Your Jesus cannot stop this rain because he is a fraud."

His response baffled me so I asked him, "Wow! Why would you call Jesus a fraud?" The man replied, "Because I've read the entire Bible from cover to cover and I know the entire Bible is a fraud! Jesus is a fraud! I was raised in a church all my life and I don't believe in any of their lies anymore!"

He went on, "Not one word in the Bible is true and I can prove it to you! The Bible is just an old book. There are thousands of manuscripts that prove the Bible is made up and full of lies to get people to conform to their way of thinking. I can prove to you that the Bible was written six hundred years after Jesus lived. And if someone tried to write down what we are talking about right now it probably would not be accurate, but if they tried to write down our conversation six hundred years from now, well, it would just be here say." He added, "That's all I want to say about that and you better get your wife back to the camper now."

"Well," I started, "I can prove to you that the Bible is true." But the man replied, "I am done talking about it! Get your wife to your camper before both of you got soaked in the rain that is coming any second now."

I said to him, "You know, in the name of Jesus I commanded the rain not to start until I walk my Jenny. And it has not started yet, has it?" The man gave me a look that said leave him alone. He said, "I already said all I'm going to say about this."

But I asked him, "Who is your source? Where does your information come from?" The man reluctantly invited me into his office to see his source. Inside, he handed me a magazine that was opened and highlighted for me to read. I told him, "I'm very sorry but I don't have my reading glasses with me." I turned to the cover of the magazine to see what kind of magazine it was. The magazine was titled AWAKE. I have never read that magazine before, so I asked him, "Who writes this Awake magazine?" He answered, "It is written by the Jehovah's Witnesses." I asked him, "You mean you would take the word of people over the inspired Word of God?" The guy told me again, "I was raised in Christian churches all my life! I don't believe any of that bull anymore!"

He said, "I know these Jehovah Witness people and they have studied for years and years and I believe they have found the truth! The truth is the Bible is a fabricated lie and I don't even believe one word of it." He said the truth is the Bible was written six hundred years after Jesus lived. He said there is just no way the Bible is true. He said again, "Now I am done talking to you so leave before you and your wife get drenched."

I replied again, "You know I ask God to hold the rain until I walk my Jenny and it is not raining on her is it?" Jenny was still sitting in the wheelchair on the road in front of the office.

I told him that I can prove to him that God is real and alive today if only you will let me pray for you. He looked at me and said, "You are not going to leave me alone until you pray for me are you?" Before I could answer him, he said again, "I told you before that I was raised in church so I know how your stupid prayer thing works. You probably have a bottle of oil in that bag on the wheelchair and you will get it and anoint me with oil and pray for me. And then when nothing happens you will say '*I guess you didn't have enough faith?*'"

I answered, "I don't carry a little bottle of oil in Jenny's personal bag on the wheel chair. But you know, that is one good idea. Furthermore, you don't need faith at all!" He looked surprised and asked me, "Where did you get that idea. You know, that is not what I was taught." I replied, "You don't need faith because you are not asking for anything so why would you need faith? I will be the one who will ask God to heal you! You see, the faith has to be in the one who is asking, not the one receiving." He looked surprised and said, "You know, that is new to me, I have never heard that before."

I continued, "So you told me that you have already read the entire Bible from cover to cover, right? So now I asked you this: how much faith did Lazarus have to come back from the dead?" The man laughed and answered, "I guess none. He was dead." I told him, "You see, the faith for Lazarus to come out of the grave had to be in Jesus because He was the one asking His Father to raise Lazarus up. Lazarus was not asking for anything at that moment. Jesus had the faith and called Lazarus out of the grave. Father God honored the faith of Jesus the man and raised Lazarus up!"

Suddenly, the man became even more sarcastic and told me, "If you are such a strong believer then, call your Jesus down here right now!" Tell Him to come right down here now and into my office now because I have some questions to ask Him right now! Come on! Call your Jesus down here or get out of my office." I replied, "You know, I don't have to call Jesus down because Jesus is standing right in front of you right now!"

He started laughing and he started to mock me, "So are you trying to tell me you are Jesus?!" I quickly replied, "No! I'm not Jesus! But I have Jesus living inside of me and I know it. Jesus is right here in this room right now. Jesus will heal you of that cancer!" He looked at me and said, "You really believe this stuff, don't you?" I said, "Yes I do because it is true and please look outside. It isn't raining on my Jenny, is it?"

The thunder was even louder and the rain was so close you could smell it and almost feel it. He said, "You will not leave me alone until I let you pray for me, will you? I said, "I really want to see Jesus heal you and I want to see you free from cancer." He looked outside at Jenny and saw that it was not raining. He put out his hand and said, "Go ahead, say your prayer. Just get it done already then leave me alone." I held his hand and commanded the cancer to go in Jesus name. He said, "I told you nothing would happen and he added I don't feel any different."

I told him, "Jesus always made the person prayed for do something they could not do before Jesus prayed. Jesus did this to prove to them they were healed. You know, like stand up and walk or open your eyes and see. I don't know what to tell you in order to prove to you the cancer is gone." He said, "I don't feel any different."

I stood there quietly for a moment and said, "Oh, I just heard Jesus say ——" The man interrupted me with laugher saying "You just heard from Jesus?" I said, "Yes! Jesus has been talking to me this whole time." He said, "So what did your Jesus say?" I replied, "My Jesus said to tell you the next time you go to the hospital for your cancer treatment, ask your doctor to do a cancer marker on your blood work." He said, "But they do that all the time. That is how they know the cancer is advancing faster than they thought. I really have less than three years to live."

I told him, "Jesus told me the next time you go to the hospital and after the doctor looked at your new blood work, you should expect the doctor to say '*why are you here?*' And at that very moment you can expect that bag to fall off too." He smiled at me and said, "You really believe that, don't you?" I said, "Yes, I do believe. Just look outside at my Jenny. It isn't raining on Jenny, is it"?

We walked out on the porch and the wind was blowing very hard. The rain was really close, but not one single drop has fallen. I turned to him and said, "I am going to prove to you my Jesus is real. I am going to walk Jenny all the way around the campground and then head back to the camper and not a single drop of rain will fall on us. He sat down in his chair and looked at me and said, "We'll see."

I walked my Jenny all the way around the campground and it took us about twenty minutes. The whole time we are walking it is evident that the rain was close by – you could smell and see it. And yet not a single drop fell on us or the campground. As we walked by him, I saw the man again sitting on his porch. I smiled and greeted him, "Good night." He watched me as I untied Jenny and carried her inside our camper.

Immediately, like that very second, the rain started to pour hard. I did not even have the door of the camper shut when the huge downpour occurred. But not a single drop fell on my Jenny. Thank you Jesus!

The next day, we left to head wherever we were going at that time. A funny thing happened every time I told that story to anyone. When I would get to the part where the man showed me the Awake magazine, people would always react the same way by saying "Oooh..." One morning, while having Coffee Time With Jesus I ask my Jesus why do people react like that when I tell them it was an 'Awake magazine.' Jesus told me they react that way because the Jehovah Witnesses people are trained to argue the Bible. I said, "But Jesus, we did not argue." Jesus said, "I know we went right for his healing."

About a year and a half later, I was going down the expressway with my Jenny and I saw that same campground. I pulled in and as I drove up to the office, I saw the same man standing on the porch and he was talking to someone. He turned and looked at my camper and had a look on his face like, "*Is that the one?*" I got out of the camper and started walking towards the office.

He recognized my face. Beaming, he started to run towards me and hugged me very tight. He told me, "It is gone! It is really gone!!!" Actually, the man is really big. I think he picked me off the ground as he hugged me.

The man couldn't stop smiling at me as he signed us up for the night. This campground has a no-wash policy – this means you are not allowed to wash your camper inside that area. But I ask if I could wash the bugs off the front of the motor home and he gave me a big smile and said you can even wash your whole camper. He added, "And if you use too much water and the grass grows I'll just send down the lawnmower tomorrow. You have clout in this campground!" We praised God and thanked Jesus!!!

Jesus has all the power and Jesus will protect you. Jesus will give you the words to say and Jesus will let His love flow through you to all, if you just make yourself available to Him. You want Joy? It is yours free if you simply ask Jesus, "What are we going to do today." I know the answer to this question is TRANSFORM A HEART TODAY. I tell you, JESUS IS REAL! His love is real and His love is for you right now! I don't try to make anything happen because I know when I focus on Jesus; my focus becomes what Jesus needs done today.

Sometime in my quiet time with my Jesus, we make up little poems.

For example, today we have written:

I live to glorify my Jesus every day;
I live to build His kingdom with the words I say.
I live to glorify my Jesus in every way;
By doing His good works today!
Transforming the world, one heart at a time is not a dream;
It is my hope in the ONE I have never seen!

With faith in Jesus I know; The Words of my Jesus will flow and devils and their evil works will go!

So today, surrender your heart to Jesus and Jesus will give you a brand new start. We can follow my Jesus and change other people's hearts into His image and likeness. We can be life to the world and dispel evil darkness. Transform this world, one heart at a time by being the love of my Jesus all the time!

Jesus Is In the Details

Jesus wants to be in every detail of our life. Jesus wants us to talk to Him and Jesus wants to be our best friend.

Yesterday, I pulled into a campground in the mountains of California. The closest grocery store is about 12 miles from here. So I went to pick up a couple things I needed. While I was there, I saw the store had a bakery. I picked up four-pack of some really good-looking coffee cake muffins. I couldn't wait to get back to the camper and have some Coffee Time With Jesus and one of these muffins. It turns out the muffins were really stale. I finished one of the four, but it was a little disappointing.

The next morning when I was having Coffee Time With Jesus, I looked at the three remaining muffins and I thought I should throw them into the woods behind my camper and let the animals have them. But before I did that, I decided to ask Jesus first what I should do with the remaining muffins. I heard from Jesus immediately, "Get a cereal bowl. Break one of the muffins into pieces in that bowl and then pour coffee on it. You'll enjoy it." I did as instructed and the taste is so great! Thank you Jesus! You even care about my muffins. They were so great I started wondering if the store had more stale ones. Jesus is in the details of your life if you talk to Him and listen for His voice.

I love you Jesus; I love you being so close to me.

Another morning when I was having Coffee Time With Jesus I noticed a woman bent down behind my car. I opened the window of my camper and asked her, "What are you doing?" She said, "I am taking a picture of your bumper sticker." The bumper sticker the woman was taking picture of says, "ABORTION" in bold black letters and right below it says "YOU ARE FORGIVEN" in red letters like the words of Jesus in the Bible.

I told the lady that I have extra bumper stickers and if she would like one I will gladly give her some. She was excited and gladly received one. We started talking and it turns out she was on three committees for the Catholic Church that are fighting abortions. She knew a lot of people who are and she herself was very active in the fight against abortions. She told me that no one she knew had taken this approach.

I told her the story of how Jesus gave me a picture in my mind of what He wanted my bumper sticker to say. The picture Jesus gave was of a white bumper sticker, like the white pages of the Bible. In bold black letters was the word ABORTION and right below were the words YOU ARE FORGIVEN, written in red like the red letters of the words of Jesus in the Bible. I said, "We both know it is the goodness of God that leads a man to repentance, not guilt, shame and condemnation. So our bumper stickers should reflect how Jesus lived and how we should live in the perfect love of Jesus." To me perfect love is the perfect forgiveness of Jesus.

She was so pleased to have one of these bumper stickers. Her husband had walked up and started talking with us along with their daughter who was going to enroll in a college today. We talked for an about two hours and then they had to leave.

I went back into my camper and noticed the garbage can was full so I decided to take it to the dumpster. As I approached the dumpster from the east, there was a man coming from the west. He had a really big smile on his face and kept it as we drew close to the dumpster. I naturally ask him, "What is up?" He continued to smile and said, "I am a pastor of church nearby, and I have asked Jesus for spiritual eyes and I can see you have the spirit of Jesus and the joy of the Lord all over you." He even brought his wife over to meet me later. He also invited me to talk in his church. We talked for about 20 minutes or so when they had to go.

I decided to go to the campground office and pray for one of their workers who fell off a ladder and hurt his back a couple weeks ago. The man was in the campground lounge and I prayed for him. As I was leaving the lounge area, an elderly man who was standing by the door asked, "How are you?" I replied, "I am blessed and I pray you are too." He said, "I'm SOS." I had no idea what that meant so I ask him, "What does that mean?" To him, S.O.S. means Same Old Sh--.

I told him, "If you know Jesus, every day would be an adventure." He looked at me sarcastically and said, "So tell me what has your Jesus done for you today?" I told him about the bumper sticker lady and being invited to speak in a church and having the privilege to pray for someone hurt. I also told him that it is only 10am in the morning so who knows what else God has for us to do today. I added, "Sir, I never feel bored. In fact, I am always excited! His look of unbelief said it all as he left. I guess some people would rather be bored (SOS) doing what they think will make them happy, rather than to give up some of their time (die to self) for my Jesus. Isn't that sad? I pray for him to come into a joy filled life with my Jesus also.

THE HITCHHIKERS

I talked a lot about asking Jesus every day, *'what are we going to do today'.* I have mentioned that most of the time I never got an answer to that question. Now, I would like to give you an example of when I heard from my Jesus after asking Him the question and you will see my Jesus in every detail.

Jesus plainly said, "Wax your camper." I thought to myself, I love how the camper is looking, because I love to tell people the story of how Jesus got it for me. I don't think the people I tell the story too would be very impressed if my camper was dirty and looking like a big mess. The story of how Jesus gave me this camper is in *Jenny's Wheelchair* book. If you need one free call me 513 377 1727

I finished my Coffee Time With Jesus that morning and then started waxing my camper. My camper was parked parallel to State Route 98, which is the main route though Carrabelle Beach Florida. There is a big grassy area between my camper and the road. I had waxed about half of one side of the camper when I stepped down off the ladder and saw three people hitchhiking out on route 98.

I knew from my hitchhiking days in the Navy it is very hard for two people to get a ride together. There were three of them and so I thought to myself they will never get a ride. Besides that, they were all wearing black clothes, which made them look mysterious. Anyway, I was able to get their attention and called them over to my campsite. They stood under the awning of my camper as I told them, "I will take you where you need to go. I just need to unload the back seat of my car first, to make room for you three." I don't believe they were used to kindness and so they asked, "How much gas money do you want?" I said, "No, I don't need any. My car gets great mileage so I don't need anything from you."

They piled in the car and I started driving west on Route 98. The man in the front seat started telling me how they had planned to spend the weekend at his girlfriend's house, but he and his girlfriend had a fight and as he put it, "the b---- threw us out." In a very short time, I was getting tired of his dirty language, so I silently ask Jesus to change the atmosphere in my car. Jesus said, "You do it." I asked Jesus, "How?" Jesus said, "Start talking about me." So I ask the man in the front seat, "How is your walk with the Lord?" The man looked at me like I had just grown two heads and three eyes.

He didn't seem to want to talk about God so he asked me, "How about you? You didn't even say goodbye to anyone in your camper before we left, so are you living in the camper by yourself because your b---- threw you out?" I said, "Yes, I am living in the camper all by myself, but not because my wife threw me out. You see, I'm by myself because my precious wife of 40 years died two weeks ago." After I said that, the man seemed out of words to say. But the girl in the back seat asked, "How did your wife die?"

I started telling her about Jenny's death and our walk with the Lord. I had only talked for a short time when she said "I have heard this story before!" I asked her, "Where?" The girl asked me if I had written a book about my Jenny and I answered "Yes." She then asked me, "Did you eat in a restaurant called *Hog Wild* last week?" And I said "Yes, I did." She said, "You gave one of your books to the waitress there, didn't you? And I said "Yes, I did." Then the girl blurted out, "Well the waitress whom you gave the book to is my sister. And she calls me every night to tell me about Jenny's wheelchair book she is reading!"

I said, "When we stop I can give you one because I have some copies in the trunk of the car. She was so happy to have her own copy and I was also happy to give her one. Hearing about someone reading Jenny's book brings such joy into my heart and then to hear about the waitress sharing Jenny's story with her sister, was like big icing on a big cake.

I continued talking about the Lord when the man in the front seat asked me to stop at a convenience store so he could get something to drink. He came back to the car with a big smile on his face and said, "You know what? My life is already changing from being with you." I asked him, "How so?" And the man answered, "I walked into the convenience store and found some money on the floor."

I had only driven about 15 or 20 miles when they had me turn down some back roads to a long gravel driveway. We ended up in a rundown mobile home with the windows broken out and the front door lying on the rotten deck so they could walk to the door to enter the house.

I gave the girl a copy of Jenny's wheelchair book and she was very happy. I said goodbye and left. Upon arriving back at my camper I started putting my stuff back in the car again. I noticed a tie dyed T-shirt was on the floor behind the front passenger seat and thought that shirt has to belong to the hitchhikers.

I drove back to the mobile home where I had dropped them off. As I drove down the gravel driveway, a man came out of the house. He was tall and kind of skinny. It was very obvious that he is proud of his tattoo's that covers his body. At least he had underwear on. He walked up to my car and said, "WHAT?" I told him I had dropped off some hitchhikers here earlier and one of them had forgotten their tie dyed T-shirt in my back seat.

At that point, one of the hitchhikers came out of the house and saw me. I told him why I came back and he was totally blown away. You see, when I offered them a ride they were trying to figure out my motive. One of them asked me how much money did I want for gas. I think he was really impressed because first of all I didn't ask for gas money and now I came all the back to give them their shirt back. I love to be a vessel for Jesus and I love when Jesus blows people away; but wait there is more, Jesus was not finished yet.

I drove back to my camper again and finished putting my stuff back in the car. There were three big motor homes camping right across from me. They were traveling together and they liked wine. I figured they liked wine because they had a decorative clock flag with wine glasses where the numbers on the clock would normally be. The flag reads ITS WINE O'CLOCK.

One of the men came over to me and asked me, "Who were those people you had in the campground?" I answered, "I didn't know them personally. I just saw them hitchhiking so I offered them a ride." He said, "So you don't know them?" I said, "Sir, I never saw them before today." He told me, "I don't like you inviting people who look like them into this campground." He went on to say, "While you were unloading your back seat they were looking around like they were casing the place." He repeated again, "I really don't appreciate you inviting those kinds of people into this campground."

I told him I was sorry if my actions upset him and I told him I would be mindful of his concerns in the future and if I see any more hitchhikers out on the highway I will go out on the highway to pick them up. He said again how seeing that kind of people in the campground looking around was upsetting to him.

Then he asked me again, "Are you sure you really didn't know them?" I assured him I didn't know them. The man told me, "So if ever I see them around here or in this campground and I call the cops, you will not be upset?" I said, "Sir, you can do whatever you need to do to protect yourself but I don't think they were casing this place."

He started to walk away, when he noticed my ladder had my waxing rag on it. He also noticed that the side of the camper had wax on half of it. Then he said, "Let me see if I have this right. You were in the middle of waxing your camper and you stopped waxing it to give people you did not know and who looked like they did; a ride to wherever they wanted to go?" I said, "That is correct." He shook his head in disbelief as he walked away.

I started waxing my camper again, when I saw him coming towards me. He said, "I noticed your camper only has a thirty amp service to it." I answered him, "Yes." He said, "I just bought my new motor home and my new one is a 50 amp service. I have a lot of stuff from my old motor home that I don't need anymore." He invited me over to see if I could use any of his stuff. I saw a lot of things I could use. I ask him, "How much money do you want for these things?" He thought for a second and said, "If you want to give me something, give me 20 dollars. After hauling the stuff to my motor home, I realized he had just given me about eight or nine hundred dollars' worth of stuff for just 20 dollars. You know you just cannot out give God! Thank you Jesus! I love you too!

Make your life an adventure by asking Jesus what are we going to do today and let the adventure begin.

The Comforter

I see people go to college and study for years to get a prestigious degree. If you want the truth, the whole truth and nothing but the truth, then let the Comforter educate you. Yes, the Holy Spirit of Jesus and Father God will walk, talk and live in you. Now that is a prestigious degree and it is living at its best.

John 14:26 But the Comforter, *which is* the Holy Ghost, whom the Father will send in my name, he shall teach you all things, and bring all things to your remembrance, whatsoever I have said unto you.

Last night, while I was visiting my friends at Lee College in Cleveland, Tennessee, we went into Chattanooga to a large church that was having a revival. There was a lot of what I call '*screaming music*' going on. They sang 'break every chain' for what seemed like fifteen minutes. The pastor called on the Holy Spirit to come down and a lot people got slain in the Spirit.

I watched a little girl, being held in her father's arms. Her pretty little smiling face suddenly changed to total fear as the pastor touched a man next to her father and the man was 'slain in the spirit'. The man fell hard to the floor and was lying on the floor for a long time; I watched as the little girl kept staring at the man on the floor. You could literally see the fear in her tiny little face. So I walked up to her and told her the man on the floor was all right and would get up again real soon. The father of the little girl smiled and said, "Thank you". The father was so focused on what was going on up front that he didn't notice the fear in his little girl.

The father handed the little girl to her mother who was also focused on the singing about breaking every chain and she didn't address the fear in the little girl either. I started to wonder, "Is this really of God? I mean that little girl did not seem to be receiving

105

the love of God in this service. On the contrary, she seemed to receive the fear of the devil."

The pastor called for people to bring their lost relatives and neighbors to the church. There was a call for parishioners to bring adulterers, homosexuals, etc. to church and the pastor proclaimed I will set them free. I could not help but to think, "Where is that in the Bible?" Jesus never told us to bring sinners to a church to have them set free. Jesus told us we are the church and as such, we are to go and preach the gospel to every nation. Jesus told us to baptize and set the captives free! I believe we are the ambassadors for Jesus and we have the Holy Spirit in us and we have the commission to go and expand the kingdom of God. Yes, we are commanded to tell everyone the Good News.

We are the church. We are the ambassadors. We have the Holy Spirit in us and we are to build the kingdom of God! The call of the Pastor was great and I understand his calling. But the problem is most people think they have done their job whenever they can get a relative, neighbor, or a sinner to the church building! I believe some people hear the pastor tell them to get the sinners to church and by doing so; they have transferred the job or work of the kingdom onto the pastor. I mean, the parishioners think I got them to church and now it is up to the Pastor to minister to them. I just don't see that in the Bible.

I believe our true calling is to be the love of Jesus to all. I believe when you ask Jesus into your heart and let Jesus transform you, you will become the love of Jesus. With the love of Jesus, you will naturally attract neighbors, relatives, adulterers, homosexuals and sinners of all kinds. They will see the purest heart of the love of Jesus in you and transformation will happen right in front of your eyes. If there are little ones present, they will receive the love of Jesus into their heart by simply hearing and watching the love of Jesus flow through you and their little ones will respond with joy instead of fear

Jesus is our Comforter and Teacher still today! We have Jesus living with us so don't worry about what to say and do, to change the heart of a sinner. For Jesus said, "Love never fails." We know we have the love of Jesus in us and His love in us never fails! We can talk to sinners knowing Jesus will give us the words of wisdom

106

to transform the heart of sinner's one heart at a time! Jesus said I will bring all things to your remembrance. He is the comforter and Jesus is comforting me.

When you give permission to Jesus to transform your heart into the love of Jesus and for Jesus to dwell in you, you are actually allowing Jesus to remove all fear, doubt and unbelief! I would call it being set free and it is the freedom to set others free. Jesus went into the sinner's houses and set them free! Jesus is our example so we are to follow Him. I cannot find anywhere in the Bible where Jesus sent or took people to the synagogue to be set free.

Another gift from God in our commission to transform hearts to Jesus is the gift of discernment. Please ask Jesus to help use your gift of discernment. Jesus said, "My people know my voice and follow my voice and a stranger's voice they will not follow." You are to be the voice of Jesus by having Jesus live inside you. To be the voice of Jesus or to be His ambassador, we must be able to distinguish the voice of Jesus from a stranger's voice. You know this is possible because we do it every day. We recognize the voice of our loved ones, even if they change their voice on purpose to trick us as a joke. I know Jesus never changes His voice to trick us but I'm making the point that if we hear the voice of a loved one, we will know the voice even if they tried to trick us.

John 10:5 Yet they will by no means follow a stranger, but will flee from him, for they do not know the voice of strangers.

The gift of discernment is something everyone is given, but not all exercise it. As you study the word of God in His Bible you will start to recognize a pattern to the will of God. The first step of recognizing the will of God will be to listen for His voice as you read in His Word you will recognize God's is loving kindness towards all. Any voice you hear in your head that would not spread loving kindness to all is not of God. Pretty simple, isn't it? God's will is truth, peace, joy, compassion and love.

HIS NAME IS JOHN

The other day, I saw a woman breastfeeding her baby in the vestibule of a church I went too. I waited until the baby was finished having breakfast and asleep before I went over and ask if I could pray a blessing over her little one. The mother of the child said yes to my request to pray a blessing for her baby. We continued talking until the whole service was over. Then, her husband and mother walked up. After introducing me to her mother, the young mother of the baby asked me to talk to her mother. I started to talk to grandma and not before long, she asked me to pray for her marriage. She said, "My husband and I are on the verge of a divorce and I don't want the divorce to happen."

I started praying and asked Jesus to give *John* discernment. The lady opened her eyes and, with amazement she quickly asked me, "Did you say John?" I said, "Yes." She said, "But I never told you His name." I said, "I know Jesus did." She was amazed and received the words of Jesus really well. I also thanked her for the privilege of praying for their marriage.

A couple days later, I was talking to a friend that pastored churches for years. When he heard this story, he asked me if I had been praying and fasting for Jesus to give me wisdom to reveal the names of loved ones while praying. I told him, "No. I have Jesus living me." When I received Jesus into me, I received the whole package. I mean Jesus is complete. I don't pray for something I already have. Simply believe you have Jesus in you and you will have all the gifts of Jesus in you. Jesus will manifest what you need when you need it. Believing is all you need and Jesus will manifest the rest or I should say His best in you."

DISCERNMENT FOR TWO DIFFERENT FAMILIES
Discernment is so necessary in life, read these two stories and see how important discernment is.

First family, A couple of weeks ago, I visited my friends in a small town in Georgia. While we were on a walk one Sunday afternoon, we ran into Bill, another friend who was also on a walk. One look at Bill and it was very easy to discern he was not doing too well. Bill started telling us about how he cannot get a job. Moreover, Bill has really bad seizures and because of this condition he has pretty much exhausted all the job possibilities in that area. Bill went on to tell me the children are hungry and they were out of food stamps. Bill's wife is now working, but she will not be paid for three days. He said his children were becoming disrespectful towards him and they couldn't understand why he couldn't get a job. Bill was totally depressed, so we talked for a couple hours about the Lord and hopefully our talk will gave him hope.

About two weeks later, Bill called me and said he needed to repent to me because he spent the money I gave him for food on beer and smokes. Bill was repenting when I stopped him and said, "You know Bill, if I were there with you on the sidewalk right now and you told me face to face how you spent the money, I would still hand you all the money in my wallet again right now." I was blessed by Jesus to tell him that God never gives up on Bill and neither will I.

While telling my encounter with Bill to a friend, my friend told me, "Ron, it would be a lot better for you to buy the children food than to hand money to Bill again." I answered him, "I see your point, but if I bought the children food, I would only be putting a Band-Aid on the problem. You see, if I buy food for the children, what am I really saying to Bill is 'I think you are such a loser and I do not trust you with the choice to feed your children or buy beer with the money I give you. You will probably never change; your repentance was not real so I will feed your children for you'. This would make Bill feel like a bigger loser."

I continued, "On the other hand, if I give the money to Bill and trust Bill with it and he chooses to feed his children, he will see the children being fed because of his decision not to buy beer. Bill will know in his heart that he made the right decision and he will be proud of himself. His children might become a little more respectful towards him. Bill will probably sit down and eat with his children, knowing he made the right choice and knowing he has done the right thing before God and man. Bill will have the Joy of the Lord in his heart watching his children happily eating. You see, if I buy the children food and they are eating in front of Bill, every time they eat Bill would be loaded with guilt and shame. Bill would probably not even want to be in the kitchen while the children were eating. I believe what Bill needs is another chance and I believe I was hearing from my Jesus to give Bill the money and trust him to feed his children.

Second family, I would like to tell you another story that happened in Denver, Colorado. Jenny and I were camping next to a young couple that had a little girl who was about 9 years old and twin boys who are about 3 years old. These children were so cute that Jenny and I had a blast just watching them. We had lived next door to them for about two weeks when they mentioned how they were living in between paychecks and they were already running out of money. They asked us if they could borrow some money until they received the paycheck from the last job the man of the house did. I mentioned to them that I needed a little job to be done on my camper and if he would help I could just give him cash. He was really happy and helped with the repair.

To my surprise that night, he and his wife had beer and smokes with friends that came by their camper for a visit. The next morning he told me he had called his last place of employment and that they had sent a check which should be here today. And guess what? The check didn't come, and the children were hungry.

I put Jenny in our car and bought some groceries for them. We were able to put the groceries on their steps and landing of their camper. They never knew for sure who bought them the groceries, but they were happy to have them, because their pay check didn't come for two more days.

The difference in the way Jesus had me handle these two families (Bill in Georgia and the one in Colorado) comes down to discernment. The last couple just made a bad choice, thinking they knew their check was coming and it was a very large check. They didn't feel the need to even repent for their bad decision because according to them the problem was not in them it was in his last boss. All I am trying to say here is we have to use discernment in every situation.

Through discernment we can transform hearts. And with relationship with Jesus, we will know the most important heart to transform is the one in front of you right now.

Jesus has been my best friend for over four years now and our relationship continues to grow. Transforming any ones heart can be a monumental job and be very time consuming. Never try to transform anyone on your own. A heart transformation back to

God can only be done through the guidance of Jesus. This is why it is so important to have your own relationship with Jesus first. If you would like to know how much Jesus loves you; I can tell you!

Matthew 18:12-14 "What do you think? If a man has a hundred sheep, and one of them goes astray, does he not leave the ninety-nine and go to the mountains to seek the one that is straying? And if he should find it, assuredly, I say to you, he rejoices more over that sheep than over the ninety-nine that did not go astray. Even so it is not the will of your Father who is in heaven that one of these little ones should perish.

This story in Matthew is really been preached a lot but just the other day, Jesus spoke to me through it saying, "Ron you are the one that went astray that I seeketh after and rejoiced of finding you." I cried as Jesus spoke these words to me. We all need to know that we are loved like this by Jesus and we are this special to Jesus.

Think for a moment about how much time we spend here on earth trying to hold onto things of the Earth because we never want to lose what we have. We have insurance for protection and we spend money on wills to direct our earthly goods fairly to our children. I can tell you this for a fact: I have more Joy knowing my Jesus would leave the ninety and nine to find me than all the happiness of earthly goods combined could bring. The coolest part is this I do not need anything to protect this Joy and I can give it away day after day and I never run out of Joy! Now that is a Jesus Joyful day!

Read Matthew 18:14 if you want to know the will of the Father, for He makes it really clear. We are the little ones that the Father does not want even one of us to perish. If someone is standing in front of you right now, tell them, "You are the one Jesus left the ninety and nine to seeketh after!" Then blow their minds by telling them Jesus is seeking after you also. I believe you will have their attention and when you tell them; Jesus will rejoice in heaven when they turn their heart to God, I believe they will receive joy beyond our understanding.

Here is an example of faith in how much God loves you: Faith is knowing Jesus loves you and knowing comes by faith that Jesus loves you. I mean, I know by faith that I am so important to Jesus and that Jesus will leave the ninety and nine just to come look for me. That is faith and I know Jesus loves me! I am the sheep that Jesus and my Father rejoiceth over. Believe me, that is some real good revelation!

I would like to ponder these Scriptures from another angle:

Matthew 18:12-13 What do you think? If a man has a hundred sheep, and one of them goes astray, does he not leave the ninety-nine and go to the mountains to seek the one that is straying? And if he should find it, assuredly, I say to you, he rejoices more over that sheep than over the ninety-nine that did not go astray.

I don't think more highly of myself because Jesus gave this revelation to me. I guess I was getting puffed up about how much Jesus loves me so Jesus spoke to me again, saying, "You know Ron, anyone of the other ninety and nine could go astray and Jesus would go find them also." Each one of us is made in His image and likeness and Jesus is so proud of His creation he doesn't want to lose even one of us.

Can you imagine yourself being a super great artist? The situation is this: your artwork becomes known around the world. All your paintings are different, but there are some similarities in your painting skills that are only yours alone and no one else can duplicate. Then, you found out that someone is going around the world and destroying your paintings one at a time. You would probably spend the rest of your life trying to protect your works of art.

Can you imagine the joy in your heart if you found your paintings being protected by someone you don't know? When you ask him why he protected your paintings, he says there seemed to be something special about them, so he just wanted to save them.

I'm telling you we are more than a work of art. We are the artwork of Jesus at work here on the earth! The devil comes to steal the artwork of Jesus and Jesus said I will rescue my artwork if they will seek after me and my joy instead of earthly junk that moths and rust will eat away.

Remember, Jesus loves us so much that He gave His life for us. Don't let the earthly stuffs move your focus away from Him! Nothing will ever compare to the perfect love of Jesus. Ask Jesus to come into your heart. Become one of His willing vessels and transform this world. One heart at a time works! Jesus said if you simply believe in Him out of your belly will flow rivers of living water. I believe when Jesus speaks of water coming out of your belly, Jesus is equating water to love. Become a river of love for Jesus and transform the heart of the person next to you today.

Joh 7:38 He that believeth on me, as the scripture hath said, out of his belly shall flow rivers of living water.

Pastor's Prayer

A couple of Sundays ago, I happened to be in a church that was full of love. Everyone seemed so happy and friendly and so was the pastor. After three worship songs, the pastor started the service by taking prayer requests. He had a notepad with him and after hearing all the requests, he started praying. He asked the Holy Spirit of God to come down and touch and heal Sister Sally, who was diagnosed with cancer earlier this week. He went through the long list of needs and for every need he ask God to send the Holy Spirit with the special healing touch of God, heal the sick or bring financial blessing to those struggling financially. He ended the prayer by thanking God for hearing our needs and sending the Holy Spirit to help and to heal the sick.

After the service was over, I waited for everyone to leave and then greeted the pastor. I mentioned to him how good the lead guitar player was and the pastor proudly said the lead guitar player was his son. I asked him, "How many children do you have?" The pastor replied by telling me, he has three children. He went on to say the other two play music, but they are just a little too shy to get up in front of the congregation. I felt prompted to ask him a question and he said he had time, so I asked.

Let us suppose it is Saturday morning and you and your wife have to go into town for the day. Before you leave the house, you tell your children to wash the car, cut the grass, clean the house, fold and put away the laundry. You tell the children when the chores are finished, the rest of the day is theirs and they can do as they will with there time. You arrived home around five o'clock in the afternoon and the children are all excited to play a new song they wrote just for you. The song is all about how much they love their mom and dad. The words are beautiful and so heartfelt. They sing with such compassion and it is obvious that they spent the entire day writing this song of love for their parents."

"After telling them how great the song is and how much you appreciate them writing a song of love for us, you mentioned that you noticed the car was still dirty and the grass was not cut and the laundry was still in the laundry room. Your children tell you they worked on the song all day, so they didn't have time to do the chores. You tell them again how much you appreciate the love song they made, but you ask them to do these chores before you left that morning and you tell them again how you made sure they had everything they needed to do the chores you gave them before you left for the day. Again you tell them go do the chores now."

"About a half hour later, you walk by their bedroom and you hear your three children praying, asking God to send the Holy Spirit down and give their dad the desire to wash his own car and cut his own grass. You hear them praying to God and you hear your son telling Jesus, how embarrassing it will be if some of my friends comes by and see him cutting grass or washing the car. You hear the girls telling Jesus, how they would appreciate if Jesus would come down here and make mom do the laundry. After all it is embarrassing to fold their brothers under clothes. You hear them begging to Jesus to send His Holy Spirit down here to change the hearts of their parents."

Then I ask the pastor if he thought God would answer the prayers of his children. I added, "After all, you are the father of these children and your commands were well within their capability to do. You gave them everything they need to do the chores you ask them to do. They chose to ignore the things you commanded them to do before you left and instead they decided to try to please you by writing you a love song.

The pastor looked at me and smiled and said, "I understand where this is going." I smiled and said, "Good, because I had no idea where the Holy Spirit was going with this story. I believe the pastor never asked the Holy Spirit to do the chores Jesus commanded us to do. Before Jesus left, He commanded us to heal the sick, raise the dead, and cast out devils. Jesus never told us to call Him down from heaven to do the work He gave us to do. Jesus gave us everything we need in one word, FAITH.

115

How much faith do we need to ask God to send His Holy Spirit down and let the Holy Spirit do the works Jesus commanded us to do? Jesus said that He will dwell in us so what else do we need. Jesus said here is my love, my life, my power and my authority just believe – for freely Jesus gave and freely we receive. Jesus freely gave us His love and our Father God gave us His love, His Son. Surely I can give Jesus and Father God my time.

Singing heart felt love songs to Jesus is a great way to worship Jesus and Father God, and I believe we are all part of the body of Jesus and we need inspiration from each other. I also believe when Jesus comes back He will be looking for Faith so let us be about the chores Jesus gave us to do. Jesus gave us everything we need to do His work before He left this world.

To transform hearts, all you have to do is hear from the Holy Spirit and let Him flow through you to others. With the Holy Spirit in you, transforming hearts one at a time is really that simple. I never feel the need to call the Holy Spirit down because I know He is already here and in me. Pretty simple isn't it? Loving Jesus and being loved by Jesus is so much more than a bus ticket to heaven. I am sure Jesus loves the songs we sing on Sunday morning, but I think we should worship Jesus by our faith. Faith is an action word and by Faith we prove we know Jesus lives in us, by faith we love Jesus, and by faith we please Jesus!

Yes, I am saved by being born again into the new life of knowing my Jesus on an intimate level I never knew existed. Believe me; Jesus is this intimate with all of His children if you let Him! Jesus says He wants to eat with us, be with us and live inside us! Jesus wants us to be intimate with him, by sharing everything.

Revelation 3:20 Behold, I stand at the door and knock. If anyone hears My voice and opens the door, I will come in to him and dine with him, and he with Me.

Please ask Jesus into your heart. Open your door to your heart. Listen, Jesus is knocking and Jesus said *"open the door; I will come in to you"*. That is you! Yes you! Jesus will come into you! Now you see why I said I don't need to call Him down. Jesus is inside of me. Jesus wants to be inside of you too! Jesus brings peace and Joy and strength and love and wisdom and relationship and understanding – and all you have to do is believe in the one that said he can never lie. Jesus said, "I will never leave you or forsake you." What else do you need? Jesus gave us the smallest and yet the greatest insurance policy ever written: *"I will never leave you or forsake you!"* Eight words of pure freedom from fear. Believe them.

We have a guarantee from God Himself and there is no fine print in God's guarantee, "I will never leave you or forsake you." Please ask Him into your heart and walk boldly and walk fearlessly. Walk knowing that the Holy Spirit of Jesus and God lives inside of you. You will be so full of Joy knowing that there is nothing in this world that can compare to a heart to heart relationship with my Jesus.

Singing songs of love and praise, waving flags in the church building are all great ways to show your love for Jesus, but if you really want to show your love for Jesus, do the chores Jesus commanded us to do before He left Earth to be with His Father – our Father. Please don't ask the Holy Spirit to do the things Jesus told us to do. Proclaim His word boldly! Confess that you are a believer in Jesus and Jesus will confess you to His Father.

Matthew 10:32 Therefore whoever confesses Me before men, him I will also confess before My Father who is in heaven.

I want to do the will of my Jesus and I really don't care what other people will think of me. I believe in Jesus and I confess my belief with boldness until the day I go to be with my Jesus! Although I want for that day to come quickly, I want more to be here on earth right now because every single day that I am here, I have the chance to be the love of Jesus to someone and I get to see Jesus transform someone's heart one at a time. I have peace and joy beyond my understanding. My focus is on Jesus and being His representative. My focus as an ambassador of Jesus is to transform this world, one heart at a time. My focus will never be on the problems of the world. I am the solution because I have the solution inside of me and I believe!

Come To Jesus as a Child

Matthew 18:14 Even so it is not the will of your Father who is in heaven that one of these little ones should perish.

Jesus tells us to come to Him as a child. The faith of a child is the purest example of faith we have here on earth. Jesus referred to Himself as a Child of God. A child knows who to call on or where to go for help when hurt. A child is teachable, reachable, and loveable. A child has no boundaries, a child has hope, a child has faith, and a child has no fear...

We adults usually have boundaries set up the moment we are approached by another adult. We usually do not have the same boundaries toward children. I think this is because we see children as innocent and children usually have very simple motives. So our guard is down. So be a child of God and let your innocence shine the pure love and the pure trust of our Father and Jesus all day and every day.

In Matthew 18:14, Jesus refers to us as little ones. Jesus said it is the will of the Father and that not one of these little ones should perish. I believe Jesus loves me and so I have the privilege to walk in the divine love of my Jesus! I have the love of Jesus to give to everyone and I have this gift of love gift wrapped in the Joy of the Lord! I know this sounds childish, but I don't ever want to grow up. I know Jesus loves me and I am childishly in love with my Jesus. Pretty childish and yet oh so simple, isn't it?

I believe it is easier for a child to win someone's heart than for an adult most of the time. I believe this is true because a child will not have an agenda or if they do it is a simple one. If a preacher announces that I am going to speak in his church and tells his congregation I am an author of three books, immediately there is a shift in the atmosphere. The congregation automatically thinks they have figured out my agenda.

They start to assume I am just there to sell books. As soon as I am handed the microphone I tell the congregation my books are totally free because Jesus has already paid for these books and there is no donation bucket. I tell them to please read them and hopefully they will touch your heart. This will change the atmosphere back to one where they can receive the love Jesus has for each one of them. I also like to tell the congregation I am the co-author of the books. I believe and I know Jesus has inspired me to right these books. I believe Jesus is the author and I am the child He asks to right them.

The heart of a child is so open and being childish as adults is to receive the love of Jesus with an open heart of a child. Jesus talks about this in Matthew 18:1-6.

Matthew 18:1-6 At that time the disciples came to Jesus, saying, "Who then is greatest in the kingdom of heaven? Then Jesus called a little child to Him, set him in the midst of them, and said, "Assuredly, I say to you, unless you are converted and become as little children, you will by no means enter the kingdom of heaven. Therefore whoever humbles himself as this little child is the greatest in the kingdom of heaven. Whoever receives one little child like this in My name receives Me. Whoever causes one of these little ones who believe in Me to sin, it would be better for him if a millstone were hung around his neck, and he were drowned in the depth of the sea.

I believe my Jesus is telling us to be humble, teachable, and loveable as a child of the Holy Spirit, and we shall be protected here on earth and be the greatest in the kingdom of heaven. I believe when we come as a child; we will see results like an adult.

Mark 9:42 But whoever causes one of these little ones who believe in Me to stumble, it would be better for him if a millstone were hung around his neck, and he were thrown into the sea.

Mark 9:42 assures me I am protected! People have accused me of being childish in my faith and I say I cannot get childish enough. I trust in the God of the universe who sent His son Jesus to show me His love. How can I not trust in my Father God and Jesus when all they want to do is to love me? The love they have for me is real and I know it! I love being loved and I love others because I know I am loved. I do not love others to please God. I already know I please God and I am loved by God and I am simply sharing His love with others to bring others into the realization of His love for them. Please read Luke 17:2 again.

Luke 17:2 It would be better for him if a millstone were hung around his neck, and he were thrown into the sea, than that he should offend one of these little ones.

I am blessed to walk without fear. I am blessed to live fearlessly. I am blessed to know my Jesus on such a personal level that my faith in the name of Jesus removes all fear. I pray for you to come to such an intimate relationship that you too can become childlike in your faith in Jesus! Be fearless by faith.

I know I can transform the world one heart at a time. By faith in the name of Jesus, I also know as you read this Jesus can transform your heart, so I know your heart will be next! I love you too, Jesus!

One more thought about these Scriptures, notice that Jesus said three times, once in Luke 17:2, then again in Mark 9:42 and again Mathew 18:6 what will happen to the person who would lead one of His little ones astray. I believe Jesus is telling us, we are protected and very pleasing to Him when we come to Him as a child full of faith that He will personally walk with us and that we can do all things with Jesus in us! So go transform a heart today by letting Jesus have His way in you. Thank you Jesus I LOVE YOU TOO!!!

THE PROTECTION OF JESUS IS COMPLETE

A while back, I walked into a church and I was standing in the back looking around to see where I wanted to sit. My eyes were drawn to a man sitting off to the side and toward the back of the church. I walked over to him and sat beside him. He had a great presence of sadness about him. He turned and looked at me and I asked if he was alright. He lifted his face so I could see him and it was obvious that he had been crying.

I asked him, "What is going on?" He replied to me, "No one in this church believes me. You see, last night the devil was literally on my chest choking me. The people of this church told me to call on the name of Jesus and the devil will flee. But I told them I did call on the name of Jesus, but the devil doesn't listen."

I asked him if he knew the Scriptures about coming to God as a child. He said he did and then he asked me, "What does that scripture have to do with the devil chocking me?" I said, "Everything." I asked him another question, "Do you know the Scripture that follows *come to me as a child*?" He replied, "No I don't." The next scripture says woe to the person, or thing that would lead one of these little ones astray for it would be better for them to have a millstone placed around their neck and be thrown into the ocean." and I added, "Than to see what Jesus is going to do to them."

I asked him, "Do you know what this Scripture says to me?" His face looked like he didn't know the answer. I told him, "I am protected totally when I come to Jesus with the faith of a child."

We are children of the most High Father God when we are born again. Forget what your earthly parents did or didn't do. Pray for them to come to know the Lord the way you do and pray for them to come to the Lord the way you are. When a child of God is hurt, he knows right where to go to get help. He knows who will protect him and look after him.

This man needed time to think so I moved to a different seat. After the music stopped, the preacher came to the pulpit and the first words out of his mouth were: This morning I heard from God and God wants me to talk to you about coming to Him as a child, with childlike faith that will move mountains and childlike faith that gives us power over the enemy. The man I talked to turned around and looked at me and said, "Did you hear that?" I smiled and said, "I believe Jesus is speaking to you through the preacher and giving you confirmation."

Simple childlike faith will move the mountains and keep the devil looking for greener pastures. Put your focus on Lord and see Him as your Father. Jesus said come to Him with full expedience and you can trust your problems are solved.

Adults will try to solve their own problems and usually only go to God when they have exhausted themselves. Children will run right to their parents and expect them to take care of their problem. Be a child again and be childishly in love with our Father and Jesus. Then you will run right to your loving Father and Brother's arms and expect His love to solve your problem.

Never again will you exhaust yourself when you know you are loved. The Joy of the Lord is our strength and our boldness and these gifts come to us gift wrapped in the Love of my Jesus. Please let Jesus wrap His arms around you and know His love for you is real.

THE STARFISH; A CHILDISH FAITH STORY YOU WILL LOVE.

After talking to some friends about transforming the world, one heart at a time, a friend from Dunlap, Tennessee told me this story. I don't know if he had a dream or saw this somewhere. The story is about a family that went on a vacation to the beach. Their 6 year old son who had never seen the ocean was fascinated by the beach, the sand and the water. The next morning, the parents woke up to see their son frantically running on the beach throwing something into the ocean. The father ran out of the condo towards his son and witnessed his little boy throwing the starfish back into the ocean. As the father looked around he saw thousands of starfish had washed up on the beach during the night.

The father told his son to stay calm. He explained, "Son, there are so many starfish here on the beach, you will wear your self out trying to throw all of the starfish back in the ocean. Seriously son, if you spent the entire day throwing the starfish back into the ocean, you will not make a difference! You will just wear yourself out trying to save all these starfish." Upon hearing this from his father, the little boy picked up one more starfish and threw it into the ocean and then looked up at his dad and said, "I bet I made a difference for that one, Daddy." I truly love the faith of a child.

By throwing the starfish back in the ocean, the little boy was giving the starfish new life! You might be thinking the starfish was already dead. Thank God no one told the little boy that. By turning away from the emptiness of the world and turning your thoughts towards giving new life and new hope in God to others, your spirit inside you will soar to the sky. Give your family new hope and joy by simply being an ambassador of the love of Jesus to your family. The only one who would tell you it is too late for peace and joy in your family is the devil. The joy in the heart of the little boy by doing what he could do; supersedes any sadness from hearing the discouraging words from his dad.

You will see that giving new life is better than thinking them to be dead already. The little boy saw the solution and not the problem, unlike his father who saw the problem and not the solution. The father was already defeated before he would even try to help. That is what the news media does to us today. The news media paints the picture so bleak that we adults are defeated before we leave the living room. I believe that is why Jesus said we must come to Him as little children. I believe children see the solution and simply do what they can do instead of being defeated and doing nothing.

You see, we are Christians and Christians are the difference between having Heaven on earth – faith of a child, Jesus lives inside of me, or hell on earth and faith in the devil, something will go wrong today. Do you realize that we Christians are the only example of Christianity on the earth? Jesus calls us ambassadors! I see people wasting their time searching for the right denomination or arguing their denomination is the right denomination. Some people are just looking for the denomination they are most comfortable with. I believe we need to live the life of Jesus here on the earth because to the person in front of you right now you are the Christ like representative of Jesus.

Christians really should not live in fear! If you have fear about anything, please check your belief in God meter. Your meter should be pegged out on the belief side. In other words, we have a choice to make. Do we believe in Jesus and the fact Jesus loves us or not? Nothing is impossible for me because I have Jesus living in me. I have childlike faith and I know if you meet me you will see

Jesus living in me. There is just no way Jesus could let me down. Jesus will never let you down either if you simply and childishly believe in Him. Jesus gets me up every day and Jesus asks me, "What are we going to do today?"

Today, Jesus might have you throwing the starfish back in the ocean. I mean, look at that story and think about the impact the little boy has in this story. He saw a need and tried to save the life of the starfish by doing what he could do. He didn't wait for a bunch of people to help. He didn't call 911. He didn't get sponsors and donations and computers to figure out the best way to save these starfish. The best part is he made a difference – even if it was to just one starfish. Who knows the starfish he did save might be the father of millions of future starfish.

If we wait for some leaders to emerge and lead America back to its Christian roots, we may be waiting a long time and we might miss the opportunity which is in front of us right now. I tell you, we can make a difference NOW! Simply believing we can transform the world 'one heart at a time' can make YOU the difference Jesus is looking for.

Can you imagine the difference in America if just one preacher would tell his congregation to turn off all television, radio and internet? If the pastor told his congregation do **not** listen to the news for one month? I can almost guarantee you that in three weeks, his congregation would be more joyful, have a better outlook on life and their joy would definitely be transforming others around them. Everyone they meet in the grocery store, at work or at play will be questioning what is going on with these people and their church.

If these same people who turned off their television and the news would also pick up their Bible and read the life of Jesus with the prospective of being, living and loving like Jesus, they will find Jesus will respond to them and talk to them because they have made time to listen to Him. Simply make a decision to turn off the television and let Jesus turn you into His love and Joy by simply seeking a relationship with Him. This is the relationship my Father God sent His Son Jesus to give us.

If that congregation will seek Jesus with this newfound free time, they will find their belief meter sky rocketed and the Joy of the Lord will surpass their understanding. Nothing will be impossible for them! Their joy will spread to their children and their grandchildren. They will see their children making good decisions and their joy meter will skyrocket. Try to get that out of a sitcom or sports station.

The little boy focused on the starfish he saved and all the ones he could save, not the ones he couldn't save. Jesus said to cast your troubles to Him. Set your heart on the things above and you will see the ones you can save. Focus on Jesus and let Jesus set the goals. By listening to the news we focus on the problem and how monumental it looks. When we focus on the news we will see how little we are compared to the bigness of the problems of the world.

Just come to God as a child with full expectation and you too will see the solution. God himself will put the answer in your hands. If the answer comes but seems too simple-minded for you or is not grandiose enough like the simple plan of *"go transform the world one heart at a time"* well, if that doesn't sound very grandiose to you, you probably need to read how Jesus the simple man transformed the world. The Bible is inspirational and Jesus was just one man who happened to know His Father loved Him! Please accept the love your Father has for you and let your Father love you because if you know your Father loves you, like Jesus knew His Father loved Him, then there is nothing you cannot do!

I believe Father God sent His Child Jesus to model a life for us; Jesus is our example and we are to follow Him. Jesus came to give us the same ambassadorship His Father gave Him. I believe I am a child of God! I believe like Jesus, I can transform the world because I am a Child of my Father God. I will make a difference even if my life only transforms one person.

Now I ask you: Where is your focus? Is it on the big, monumental problem? Or is it on the solution, however simple the solution may sound? Jesus said the faith of a mustard seed will move a mountain. Do you think Jesus said that because He knew we would never have monumental problems? I believe Jesus said that because He knew how big the news media would make our problems look! Read the life of Jesus and notice that Jesus never took on the challenges of the government of His day. Jesus changed the government by transforming the hearts of the people in government.

Jesus is the giver of life. Jesus is the hope for the hopeless. Jesus is the solution and the Holy Spirit of Jesus lives inside of me right now. What does that make me? Ask Jesus to live inside you and you too will become the solution!

The boldness of Jesus is a form of meekness and humbleness that flows from us Christians who will come to God as a child looking for a solution. The opposite of humbleness is pride and pride will make us look to ourselves to solve the problems of the world. Actually, pride will make you feel important and puffed up, but pride will never make you feel childish. Pride is a Band-Aid! You see transforming hearts into boldness, meekness, and humbleness of Jesus is the solution! Just become childishly in love with my Jesus and watch His childish love for you grow and overflow.

We never have to look for a problem. They exist everywhere. The only solution the news media has is that there is no solution at all. They always make the problems look really big and complicated. At best, what they offer are band aids. Isn't that ironic? We watch the news every day and stand by helplessly as our country is falling apart. We might even pray that our politicians come to their senses and do the '*right thing*'. We should be praying and thanking God for giving us the solution already. The solution is to model our life after Jesus. If we do, even the politicians will be affected or should I say infected by our Jesus virus.

You might be wondering what I am talking about when I say *Jesus virus*. I call it that because for me, the Jesus virus is a good virus. In Ohio, when the children return back to school, most will come down with a flu virus. Now, we even have flu shots to help stop the flu virus. I personally have never seen a flu virus, nor do I know how it spreads across the U.S., but I have had the result of the flu. Unlike the flu that makes you sick, the Jesus virus is the answer that makes you well from head to toe! The Jesus virus is infectious, contagious and outrageously wholesome for everyone who comes into contact with the carrier.

Think about Hitler for a moment. If one Christian had demonstrated the true love of Jesus to Hitler, (gave him a big dose of the Jesus virus) the world would not have gone through what it did and the world would not have lost all those lives. When you make yourself available to Jesus to transform a heart, you never know what that person has turned away from! Just think how your seemingly small act of kindness could have transformed a future Hitler in the making.

Think how different the world will be if one true loving example of Jesus Christ gains access to President Obama and transforms his heart! Jesus is the hope and I have Jesus living in my heart, speaking through me. And knowing that Jesus is alive in me makes me hope for a better world. I love my Jesus and Jesus loves me and together we are setting the captives free! This hope in my heart believes that we can change this world, one heart at a time! THANK YOU JESUS!!! My prayer for our country is for real true Christians to come into contact with our president real soon and for the love of Jesus to transform the heart of our president and other elected officials.

The Cutter

Over a year ago, I was introduced to Jack (not his real name). He is a man who was known as a *cutter*. A cutter is someone who will take a razor knife and cut himself. He thinks the pain of cutting himself will help him get rid of the pain from his terrible childhood. He seems totally normal for a while but when he starts hearing from the devil, he will listen to those demon thoughts and he allows the demon thoughts to take over his mind.

As things escalate, he will actually take a razor and will start to cut himself. There doesn't seem to be any help from doctors as of yet. The drugs they gave him aren't stopping the voices he hears and so the cutting just goes on.

You might be thinking, "Ron you are wrong on this one." I know some people who don't like to think that devils are talking to them but I assure you we have all heard from the devils. Any time you sin, you have heard from a devil and you have done what the devil said. I know for a fact that no one in the kingdom of heaven has ever told someone to sin, and no one in the kingdom of heaven would tell someone to cut yourself with a razor to stop your pain. I prayed for and continue to stand in faith for discernment for Jack. I know that my Jesus wins and so I have great expectations for Jack.

The third time I went to his house to talk to him, I was disappointed because he was drinking. He still seemed somewhat coherent so I stayed and talked to him until 6:00 P.M. As I left him, I noticed he was opening another beer. Around 2:30 in the morning, my phone rang. I woke up to see his number on my caller ID. I thought to myself, "I hate talking to drunks because they never remember what you say anyway." So I just let his call go to voice mail and I went back to bed. Right as I put my head on the pillow, Jesus talked to me. Jesus asked me a question, "Ron is my line ever busy?" I got up immediately and called Jack back. To my surprise, he was not drunk but he had a razor and was going to cut himself. Thank you Jesus; Jack heard from Jesus and decided to reach out for help before he started cutting.

I have no training in what to do in such cases, so I totally rely in my Jesus to be my guide. Jack talked about why he was going to cut himself so I just listened until he gave me a chance to talk. I felt prompted so I asked Jack if he still had the papers I left with him the first time I met him. I ask him to read the one titled *Coffee Time With Jesus* and he asked me why? I told him I could not remember what I wrote about in it. He started laughing and said, "You wrote this and you cannot remember what it says?"

He started reading it to me and started laughing again. He commented, "You cannot spell can you?" As he continued to read Coffee Time With Jesus to me, he told me to bring my computer up there and he would correct the misspelled words for me. He talked and laughed all the way through it. Around 5 in the morning he told me that he wanted to go to bed and so did I. He said, "I love you man" and I assured him, "We love you too." He asked me, "Did you say 'we'?" I answered him, "Yes. Jesus and I love you more than you know."

I woke up around 8 in the morning and was feeling totally rested. I had some Coffee Time With Jesus and told Jesus to flow through me any time day or night. I thanked Jesus for telling me to call Jack back that night. Most of all, I thanked Jesus for being my very best friend and for loving me so much. No one and I mean no one could love me more.

I have people tell me all the time that they never hear from God. I believe that soon Jesus will have me write a story about hearing His voice. The Bible calls it a still small voice, and it is sometimes. Like in the story above, I heard the voice of Jesus say "Is my line ever busy?" After that I was just prompted! I mean, Jesus didn't say, "Okay, now ask him to read Coffee Time With Jesus." I just felt a prompting to ask Jack to read Coffee Time With Jesus.

Jesus uses different ways to communicate with us. Prompting is a very good way to hear from Jesus because it takes faith to know you heard it right. Through listening to His voice, we will know God's will and through discernment we recognize His voice, God can use you to transform other people's hearts. I tell people all the time I never ask God where I am going or what should I do. I just simply know by faith that if I am going the wrong way Jesus will turn me around. Jesus said that without faith it is impossible to please him.

When I decided not to answer Jack's call that night, I was hearing from the devil. Jesus turned me around when He said, "Is my line ever busy?" I am so blessed to know I am loved by God!

Charity

I want to tell you a story about charity and the gifts of the Holy Spirit. I was in Minnesota with two friends and we stopped at a Vineyard church. We were early for a Wednesday night service. My friend, Pastor Joel from Cincinnati knew the pastor there. My Jesus works out every detail for me, as it turned out the youth pastor asked Joel to speak to the young teenagers. But Joel's voice kept cracking so Joel asked the pastor's permission for me to speak.

The church service started with a three minute movie about 9/11. I believe Allen Jackson was the country singer in the movie, who asked the question, "Where were you when the planes flew into the twin towers?" He ended the movie quoting a Bible verse: "There is faith, hope and love but the greatest of these is love."

When I was asked to speak to these teenagers, I asked them if they realized Allen Jackson had misquoted that Scripture. I told them that my Bible says:

1 Corinthians 13:13 And now abides faith, hope, charity, these three; but the greatest of these is charity.

I then asked these young men and women, "What do you think of when you hear the word charity?" A young girl answered *with giving* and another girl answered *with sacrifice*. I said, "Both of you are correct. To my Jesus, love is charity, caring, giving and sacrifice. When we Americans think of the word love we usually think of 'I love you. Do you love me?' So many times we think of love as a two-way street of giving and receiving or giving just to receive something in return."

I continued, "To my Jesus, charity was never about receiving! To Jesus, love or charity was always about giving. To Jesus, the ultimate giving is dying to our self! Jesus calls us into a life of dying to our self and Jesus proved it to be possible by giving all that He had. Jesus even gave His physical life for us."

John 15:13 Greater love has no one than this, than to lay down one's life for his friends.

"In John 15:13, we see the greatest love we can give or sacrifice to another is our own life like Jesus did." I looked at them and asked, "What does it look like today to give our life back to Jesus? I tell you this; today life is measured in time. Simply give God our time! Simply give God respect! Simply give God control of our life by simply listening for His voice! Simply dying to our self is asking God 'what are WE going to do today.' The life of Jesus was so simple because He simply gave up His time here on earth to do the will of our Father."

I mentioned before the service started, I noticed the information on the tables at the back of the church showed me you are all going on a mission trip to Africa. Looking at all of you, it is very easy to see you are all excited and really looking forward to going. I asked you this: Do you realize you are a fine example of John 15:13? Yes, you are actually laying down your life to go to Africa. You are giving up the things you might have done if you stayed here. You might not see yourself as giving up anything, but to the person that would say I won't go because of whatever; that person is putting their needs over the needs of the people in Africa."

Then I asked them if they realize they are on a mission trip every day. "Right here in America we can be on a mission trip everywhere we go. The requirement Jesus wants from us is to die to our self. In other words, Jesus wants us to make ourselves available to Him every day, not just on a special trip to Africa. Missionary work is not just an event. Missionary work is being and flowing the love of Jesus to everyone, every day. To accomplish this all we have to do is ask Jesus 'what are WE going to do today?' Isn't that simple?"

132

When we ask Jesus 'what are WE going to do today' we are really telling Him we are available to Him. We are telling Jesus to use us and transform us into His image and likeness. We are asking Jesus, 'let Your love flow through us like the river of living water you talk about in your word'. Read the Words of Jesus in His Bible and see the example of love flowing like a never ending river. We are to model our life by the example Jesus set and we should only do what we have seen our Jesus do.

Joh 7:38 He that believeth on me, as the scripture hath said, out of his belly shall flow rivers of living water.

I believe in Jesus and I know for a fact that I cannot flow rivers of living waters out of my belly, but with faith in my Jesus I can do all the things Jesus said and did. I cannot see love (living water) flow from me, but I can see the effect of love flowing from me. To be a missionary, all we need to know is Jesus loves us! For when we know Jesus loves us, we can be the love of Jesus to others. Isn't that simple

The realization of knowing Jesus loves us has to come first. Jesus said, "Come follow me. Jesus didn't say go try to make me love you. Jesus did not say I will love you if you go do this missionary trip for me. Do not try to earn the love of Jesus because you will be trying in your own strength and you will wear yourself out or backslide.

If we are doing missionary work to prove we love Jesus then we will probably become backsliders and give up at some point. Coming into the realization that Jesus loves us will enable us to do missionary work very effectively. To be the river of His love to others is coming in to a heavenly realm of peace and joy in this world that Jesus talks about. You know – Heaven on earth! Jesus is right. We can live in Heaven right now.

What will be the biggest revelation to you when you go to heaven? The answer; is how much Jesus loves you! The coolest thing about the love of Jesus is we can and do experience His love right now! (Heaven on earth). We have been given the privilege of giving His heavenly love to everyone right now!

Missionary work is being the love of God to everyone, everywhere, everyday. To be a missionary for Jesus, all we need is to think like Jesus. Jesus in His Word told us what to think about:

Philippians 4:8-9 Finally, brethren, whatever things are true, whatever things are noble, whatever things are just, whatever things are pure, whatever things are lovely, whatever things are of good report, if there is any virtue and if there is anything praiseworthy— meditate on these things. The things which you **learned and received and heard and saw in me,** these do, and the God of peace will be with you.

Notice that Jesus said we have both learned, and received, and heard and seen in Jesus. Please notice these are the things we are to DO. What is the reward for learning of Jesus, receiving of Jesus, hearing from Jesus, and seeking Jesus, and the GOD OF PEACE SHALL BE WITH YOU!

Seek Jesus by thinking about the things in Philippians 4:8. All these thoughts are thoughts of love. Who is love? Jesus! How do we have love living inside us? Ask the Holy Spirit of Jesus and Father God to live inside of you. Simply do these things and the God of peace shall be with you here on earth and now and forever.

I believe some missionaries become so overwhelmed by the living conditions in other countries. The most important tool to a missionary is faith. If we focus on the problem, then we are doomed. If we focus on Jesus by thinking from a pure heart of love for Jesus and if we have asked Jesus for His eyes then we will see as Jesus sees. Then we will be great missionaries because we will see the solution to the problems, not just the problems and the God of peace and joy shall be in you. Remember, you have the answer in you so just let Him flow and let Him show.

These young missionaries were ready to go to Africa and be the love of Jesus and now they knew they could be the love of Jesus everywhere and every day. Jesus says in His Bible, it is the goodness of God that will lead a man to repentance. We as Christians are to manifest the goodness of God everywhere. It is His goodness that will lead a man to turn away from sin, but no one will see His goodness unless we become His goodness. Jesus also said in His Word what we set our minds on is what we will become.

Matthew 6:21 For where your treasure is, there your heart will be also.

The goodness of God is my treasure. God's goodness is forgiveness, hope, and charity to all from your a pure heart. When we asked God into our heart and we seek God with our whole heart, God will reward us with His treasure and His pure love so we can give His pure love to one another.

Even if the problems in the foreign country are rooted in sin, you can give them the love of Jesus by being an example of the love of Jesus and Jesus in you wins the battle. Your missionary work will be a success!

MISSIONARY TRIP AT A GAS STATION

Today I met a brand new born again Christian girl who told me this story. When she stopped to gas up her car, she naturally chose the shortest line. The guy in front of her was getting into his car to leave as she pulled up. When this guy saw her waiting, he got out of his car and started to wash his windows. He seemed to be intentionally going out of his way to take up time. She said he kept looking at her to see if she was getting mad. This brand new Christian said she wanted to blow her horn and tell him to move, but she thought, "I am walking with the Lord now and how would Jesus handle this?" She thought, "I will just pray for him to finish faster." As she prayed, the guy suddenly got back into his car and left. She said he left so fast there was even water on half of his rear window. She started praising God and could not stop smiling.

I thought to myself how great an illustration of how the devil works. You see, if she had listened to the devil and blown her horn the man might have taken even longer and he may have even gotten some happiness knowing he just made someone mad. Because she sat quietly and heard the voice of God, she prayed and he decided to leave because killing someone else's time is not fun unless you can make them manifest mad. In reality, the devil in him wanted to see if the devil could get back at her, I mean she said she was a brand new Christian.

I believe the devil is looking to manifest his evil spirit everywhere, if we listen to him. He wants us to get frustrated and mad and acting out his meanest. Then, he is happy and we are not. But when we hear the voice of God and we don't get mad and frustrated, he leaves to find easier people to toy with because he gets mad and we are not. You see, she simply put the situation into the hands of God when she surrendered it to Him and then let God be God. Then suddenly the man got back into his car and left.

The man was simply listening to the devil who told him to rob the girl waiting for gas of her time. His action looked innocent; I mean he was just washing his windows. The gas station even supplied stuff needed to wash his windows. Clean windows could be a blessing from God. What changed his desire for clean windows into an act of the devil is when he looked to see if she was frustrated. Jesus said the eye is the window to the soul.

Matthew 6:22 The lamp of the body is the eye. If therefore your eye is good, your whole body will be full of light.

She could see in his eye the evilness of his desires. His motive was not to clean windows for clearer vision. The motive was to frustrate the person behind him. He had no idea she was a brand new Christian, but the devil in him did. The devil tempted Jesus right after Jesus was baptized. Why? When Jesus came out of the water His Father said, "This is my beloved Son in whom I am well pleased." The devil heard the words spoken over Jesus the man and wanted to see if Jesus the man believed it. The devil heard the confession of this girl to give her heart to the Lord and the devil wanted to see if she believed it. Jesus the man was protected by His Father and we are protected by Our Father also, right from the moment we give our heart to God. Just focus on Jesus and problem solved.

We are to be the love of Jesus here on earth today and every day. In fact, we are commanded to love with all your heart and with a good conscience and with faith unfeigned.

1 Timothy 1:5 Now the purpose of the commandment is love from a pure heart, from a good conscience, and from sincere faith

Wow! Jesus said a lot with very few words: For God, love is charity. For most of us, a pure heart would seem impossible and yet it must be possible – for Jesus is telling us that we must have a pure heart. Jesus also said that we are to have a good conscience – meaning to love without reservations, to give without judging and not expecting a return.

Faith unfeigned is what makes our heart pure and our conscience clear. Faith unfeigned is a sincere faith in Jesus. I believe the more sincere I am in my faith, the more Jesus can unlock my heart and purify me. I believe we have a natural tendency to protect our hearts and it takes faith in the protection of Jesus to make our heart open to be the love of Jesus. I believe our faith is the measure of our pure heart and good conscience.

I believe a pure heart would be impossible without faith. Also, a good conscience is impossible without faith. Jesus said that all things are possible to those that believe and I believe Jesus has a cleanup crew and they are cleaning me daily. I pray you don't need the crew as much as I do but by faith I know Jesus is cleansing me.

I start my day being conscious of God and what He needs to be done today. I believe my simple faith of allowing Jesus to have the keys to my heart and I give Him my keys with nothing held back. I give Jesus the permission to give me His thoughts, His heart, His mind and His eyes. And by faith, I receive it all; plus His joy that surpasses my understanding. Jesus is a complete package – receive the completeness of Jesus by simply seeking to know God with all your heart.

You see how simple that is? I simply ask Jesus to be the ruler of my life. You know, I just give Him the permission to make me His ambassador and in doing so I am giving Him permission to make me into His image and likeness. Here is a simple way to measure how you are doing: the more Jesus you become, the more His Words will come out of your heart. At the end of the day, sit in quiet reflection and let Jesus speak His words of encouragement to you. And you will see how His words have become your words and you will be the Jesus encouragement to everyone you met. Quite time with Jesus at the end of the day is superior to worldly news!

Here is a short story that happened yesterday: I was walking up to the campground office when I saw a woman who had an outdoor booth with some stuff for sale. I greeted her, "Hi! How are you?" The young man standing next to her answered. He said, "I'm having a rough day." He went on to say that some boys were calling him hurtful names. He said, "My dad is a preacher and he tells me to just ignore them." I said, "That is good advice, but you know you could and should pray for those boys." He asked, "Why should I pray for them. They are mean to me so I don't like them." I asked, "Would you call them hurtful names?" He said, "No."

I continued, "I didn't think you would call anyone hurtful names because I can see you know Jesus. If you pray for them to know Jesus, they will stop calling you names and as they come to know Jesus they will become your friends. I'm sure your dad will tell you how prayer changes the hearts of others, just like the love of God in you will not let you call those boys names. Pray for them to know the love of God as you do and they will not be able to call you hurtful names. In fact, if you pray for them to come to know God all their hurtful ways will disappear."

"You know, with Jesus in you there is nothing you cannot do. So pray for them to fall in love with God and God will transform them into friends for you. Jesus will flow His love through you into them when you ask Him to in your prayers."

He walked away, with his head down but I knew he was thinking about the love of God and how God's love will transform those boys and that is success.

Truthfully, we can be adults in this kingdom, yet we are still little children of our Father God. We are made in the image and likeness of God and Jesus. Jesus never told anyone to ignore a problem. Jesus never ignored our problems. The hurtful children in the story above are lost to the image God created them to be. They are lost to the power of the love of Jesus. We Christians need to invite Jesus into our life, our heart and our mind. For when we do, we will see Jesus transform children and adults alike into a life of loving others by simply letting the love of Jesus flow like a river

He Himself said we should be. I believe Jesus! I love Jesus! I love Jesus living in me! I love Jesus making me all I can be. I love Jesus talking through me and I love seeing the love of Jesus transform the heart of people around me.

Simply give permission to Jesus to transform your heart and He will. Then you will see His love and words come from you to change the heart of the ones around you. All it takes is a little faith.

Amazing Faith

Jesus said without faith it is impossible to please Him.

Hebrews 11:6 But without faith it is impossible to please Him, for he who comes to God must believe that He is, and that He is a rewarder of those who diligently seek Him.

The other day, I received a telephone call from my dear friend Alyssa. Her children call me Grandpa Ron. Alyssa has two children – Danton, who is almost five now and has been diagnosed with Down syndrome and Nakita, who is almost three. To help pay the bills, Alyssa babysits a six-month old baby. While Alyssa was occupied feeding the baby she was babysitting, Danton figured out how to open the front door of the house and got out. Within minutes, Alyssa noticed that he was missing and she went after him. A police officer was making a routine round in the neighborhood and had seen Danton all alone. The officer was trying to talk to Danton when Alyssa came running up to them.

The police officer gave Alyssa a ticket for child endangerment and actually wrote on the ticket. His reason for the ticket was Alyssa talked to Danton like he was a normal person. When Alyssa called me on the phone, it was evident that she was very upset.

Jesus is so cool. Jesus had just been talking to me about faith that morning. Hebrews 11 is the 'who's who' of faith in the Bible. I ask you, how did the men of Hebrews 11 prove they had great faith? The proof of their faith was in their trial. Without the trial, faith is just talk.

Alyssa has great faith! Alyssa has a great relationship with God and all she needed was a gentle reminder of her faith to believe God will handle this situation also. I felt prompted by my Jesus and started talking about Paul and Silas.

Acts 16:24-32 Having received such a charge, he put them into the inner prison and fastened their feet in the stocks. But at midnight Paul and Silas were praying and singing praises to God, and the prisoners were listening to them. Suddenly there was a great earthquake, so that the foundations of the prison were shaken; and immediately all the doors were opened and everyone's chains were loosed. And the keeper of the prison, awaking from sleep and seeing the prison doors open, supposing the prisoners had fled, drew his sword and was about to kill himself. But Paul called with a loud voice, saying, "Do yourself no harm, for we are all here." Then he called for a light, ran in, and fell down trembling before Paul and Silas. 30 And he brought them out and said, "Sirs, what must I do to be saved?" So they said, "Believe on the Lord Jesus Christ, and you will be saved, you and your household." Then they spoke the word of the Lord to him and to all who were in his house.

Alyssa and I talked about the faith of Paul and Silas over the phone. They did not pray to God with an answer in their heart like 'God, get us out of here or we need a lawyer or God change the hearts of the people that put us in here'. Paul and Silas simply sang praises to our Lord out loud so the other prisoners could hear them. They had faith that God would answer them. They did not surmise what the answer might be. They simply knew God had an answer and stood in faith that God would give them an answer.

Talk about faith! They knew when the earthquake shook the inner prison until the doors opened and their bands were loosed. Their faith was so strong that they didn't run out of the prison. They just stayed to preach to the other prisoners. They were in the inner prison and their faith was so strong they knew the earthquake was the answer from God and so they had no fear of the whole prison collapsing on them.

They stayed and preached to the prisoners and even saved the life of the guard and converted him and his family. Upon hearing about the faith of Paul and Silas, Alyssa's faith rose up and fear left immediately. I could hear her faith as she spoke on the phone for she already knew to sing praises to God in all circumstances.

Jesus said that without faith it is impossible to please Him. I know the faith of Alyssa pleases God and I believe God has a great reward for Alyssa's faith! I believe God and His angels are preparing a chapter in Hebrews 11 for Alyssa. And I cannot wait to read it!

Alyssa is going to have a trial by jury. She could be finished with this whole problem by simply pleading guilty before the judge but she chose not to do that. I believe she made the right choice and now will have a chance to testify before 12 jurymen and a judge. I know for a fact that she will testify of the love of Jesus to them and they will find her not guilty.

Here is another story about faith. This one is about hearing from God in a different way. I referred to this story earlier in this book, but this time from a Faith in action prospective.

Some time ago, I was in another campground. I met a man that was really well-versed in the Bible. We were talking about God and this man could quote Scripture like I had never heard. He was like a *walking, talking Bible*. In our conversation, he called me a man of God a couple times. The way he references me 'man of God' made me a little uncomfortable.

He then quoted a passage from the Bible and asked me if I could tell him what it meant. But I had no idea what it meant so I read the passage out loud from my Bible, thinking I might understand it if I read it. He said he had heard it preached in three different ways and started to tell me his version of what he thought it meant. But his explanation was very confusing to me so I said let me go to my Source and see what Jesus says about this passage.

I said out loud, "Dearest Jesus, what are you telling us in this passage?" I waited a couple minutes and heard nothing. The man waited and then asked "What did your Jesus tell you?" and I replied "Nothing." The man repeated what I said, "Nothing?" I said, "I didn't hear from my Jesus." He smiled and his face seemed puffed up with fulfillment, like he had stomped Jesus.

He then asked me rather smugly, "What do you do if your Jesus doesn't answer you?" I said, "Jesus did answer me by not answering me. When Jesus doesn't answer me, I know the answer is not important for me to know *right now*. If the answer was important to me to know right now, then I would have received the answer. My Jesus is all-knowing, and I guess I really don't need an answer right now."

We talked for a couple minutes and he left the camper. I sat quietly and asked my Jesus why I didn't hear from Him. And Jesus spoke to me right away. Jesus said, "Because all the man wanted to do was argue." I said, "Jesus you never argue. I love you Jesus, I love how you protect me from evil!" I tell you that Jesus will protect you from all evil, even useless conversations. 1 Timothy 1:4 says:

> **1 Timothy 1:4** Nor give heed to fables and endless genealogies, which cause **disputes** rather than godly edification which is in faith.

I believe Jesus never argued to win anyone over to His pure heart. I believe Jesus is telling me there is no reason to argue, just show them the love of Jesus and let Jesus bring the increase. When people see the pure heart of Jesus, they will either melt or run away.

I want to share one more thought about this story. I hope you realize that only Jesus has all the answers. Jesus has to be our source and if there are times when you don't hear from Jesus the answers to the questions we are asking; just rest knowing it is not necessary for us to know right now. No one on earth needs all the answers. Answers are knowledge and Jesus said knowledge puffs us up, but the love of Jesus edifies us! Be an edifier of love that flows from Jesus to everyone. Remember, the love of Jesus will transform the heart, not our love, not our knowledge, not our understanding, not our arguing, but simply the love of Jesus in us will transform hearts. Ask Jesus to let you become His love and Jesus and everyone in heaven will rejoice as another soul is transformed. I love how you love me Jesus.

Make my Jesus your Jesus and watch him protect you, love you and let Jesus give you His increase so you can overflow His love to all. It really is that simple. I love my Jesus and I will follow my Jesus and I prove it by simply making myself available to Him. "Good morning Jesus and what are WE going to do today"

In a letter to the Galatians, Paul wrote:

Galatians 6:8 For he who sows to his flesh will of the flesh reap corruption, but he who sows to the Spirit will of the Spirit reap everlasting life.

You see here we are to sow to the spirit. Actually, we are commanded to sow to the Spirit. To sow in the spirit, we simply live the life Jesus modeled to us every day. We don't use our Bible knowledge to stomp people or to belittle them and make ourselves look smart. When we focus on Jesus and learn to hear His voice, we will walk and sow in His spirit. I believe in the story above, Jesus sowed to the man's spirit because Jesus never argues. Arguing is fleshly and of the flesh we only reap corruption, but of the spirit we reap life everlasting. I love the way Jesus will protect you when you are surrendered to Him.

I have heard of people who will not sow at all because they are worried about themselves (pride) and they think if nothing happens (like a healing) they perceive they will look like a fool. I wonder if they have been taught or even heard about dying to self. You see, when we know Jesus is in us and we pray for people it is impossible for nothing to happen. We don't always see into the spiritual realm, but things do happen in the spirit when we speak.

When we speak words of love over people, something in their spirit will respond inside them. Like a friend of mine, Dan said at the very least you gave them a big dose of the love of God. I think our words of God's love are like pouring Miracle Grow on flowers. We cannot see anything physically different happen to the flowers immediately, but we know in our spirit, our flowers will respond with big blooming flowers in a couple days.

When we pray for others, we are actually giving them a big dose of God's Miracle love. And by faith, we know God will bring the increase. By faith, we know He will honor His Word. Be humble and pray for someone today. Jesus is looking for a willing vessel to flow through and you can be his vessel. It is an honor and a privilege to be used by God and all we do to receive this honor and privilege is fall in love with our Creator instead of the creation.

You alone cannot make it happen. But with God's Spirit dwelling in you, all things are possible! Please sow in the spirit the love of God and you will reap life everlasting. We can live in the Joy of the Lord now. The coolest thing is the person you prayed for was touched whether you saw it or not. The joy of the Lord is in them also.

SOWING THE SEED OF GOD'S LOVE

A couple of years ago, Jenny and I were in North Carolina. One day, I realized that we were close to the Billy Graham museum. I would like to say the modesty of the museum was overwhelming. While we were there, I saw a picture on the wall of an old man. The caption under the picture told a story. When Billy was only 16 years old; he had a new driver's license, when the old man in the picture asked Billy to go to a revival with him. The revival was scheduled on a Friday night and Billy had plans to go to a party. For Billy, going to this party seemed way better and more exciting than going to a revival. So the old man enticed Billy by telling him he could drive his car if Billy would come to the revival. "The revival was about thirty miles away, if I remember correctly."

The thought of driving the car enticed Billy and he agreed to go to the revival. From this revival, Billy heard the calling of Jesus to follow Him. The night of the revival, Billy gave his heart to the Lord. I'm sure neither Billy nor the old man knew where that night would lead them. You see when we sow to the Spirit by giving from our spirit and letting the Spirit of God give the increase; precious hearts are changed. Think how different the world would be if the old man would have listened to the devil that probably told him 'don't ask that wild kid named Billy; he is just a ruff teenager and wants to party tonight'.

Sowing the seeds of God's love is the best sowing any of us can do. We don't choose who to give them to – we just sow wherever we are and to whoever God puts in our path. We sow by faith and know by faith God will bring the increase. By faith we are to be at peace in the love of God and not striving to make something happen.

SOWING IN THE SPIRIT

A couple years ago, Jenny and I went to Cincinnati to visit our sons. I had just set up and hooked up our camper when a call came in from a man I met a year ago. I had not talked to him for about a year. He called and asked me to pray for his daughter. He went on to tell me that she had cancer and she will be released from the hospital the next day. The doctors told her she only had four days to live.

I met them the next day and talked to her for an hour and a half and she was amazing. She told me, "If God takes me home, I will be in heaven with him and if God lets me live here on earth I will be with my children and husband. I'm fine with whatever His decision is for me." She was totally surrendered to the will of God. She was totally at peace with what we call death or life.

Four days later, I received a phone call from her father and he said his daughter passed away that morning. After talking to him for a couple minutes he told me, he had other people to talk to. "I was not upset about her dying, but I was feeling melancholic all morning. I kept thinking about her two teenage sons and how they would grieve. I thought about her loving husband and her loving family. It was very hard for me to believe she was gone."

The day she went to be with Jesus, the weather was extremely hot and humid. I could go outside and sweat in just a couple minutes. I initially had planned to grill out that day, but because of the heat, I knew I would not be able to have Jenny out of the camper. Jenny was very temperature sensitive – she could go into a seizure real easy. I decided to take Jenny to her favorite fast food place that served chicken. Jenny could not talk, but when I feed her this chicken she would chew her food with enthusiasm.

We went to Lee's Chicken and to my surprise we were the only ones there. I ordered our meal and fed my little Jenny and as usual, she loved her meal and her smile brought great joy to me. I did not use her wheelchair; I just carried her in and out of the restaurant. As I put Jenny in the car seat, I noticed someone had walked up behind me. I turned around and there stood an older couple. The lady beamed at me, saying, "Do you know you are my hero?" Her message surprised me and I asked her, "Why am I your hero?"

She replied, "You don't recognize me, do you?" I said, "I am very sorry but I don't recognize you. Do I know you?" She told me how last year she and her husband were in the restaurant and it was very crowded but they saw me feeding Jenny from a distance. She said how they were impressed with the way I would touch each piece of food on my lip to test the temperature of the food before I would give Jenny a bit.

She went on to tell me, "How all of a sudden I turned around and looked about like I was looking for someone. Then you propped up your wife in the corner of the booth very carefully, so she could not fall and you stood up and walked right to our table."

She continued, "You saw my deformed hand and ask if you could pray for it to be healed." Then I said to her, "I remember you now because you told me I could pray, but you started to pull your hand away when I reached for it." She said, "Yes that is right." I put my hand on hers and prayed for healing and thanked God for doing it. She told me no one had ever prayed for her to be healed before.

She told me, she was surprised that I would pray out loud in the crowded restaurant for her. Anyway, nothing happened physically so I just thanked her for letting me pray for her. Now, while standing in the parking lot, she pulled her hand out from behind her back to show me and tell me how the next day when she got up her hand was perfectly healed.

She said, "My husband and I have been going to this restaurant at least once a week for over a year now. And we have driven through the parking lot a couple times a week also to try to find you and to tell you about the miracle." We hugged and laughed as we talked about how good my Jesus is. Then she asked me, "Will you pray for my husband? I replied, "Sure. What is going with you, Sir?" He said he had colon cancer and was going for treatments five days a week. I prayed for him and commanded the cancer to go in the mighty name of Jesus. I then pronounced to him that the cancer is gone.

He said the doctors told him the cancer is going into remission, to which I replied "Jesus does gone, not remission." He looked at me like I was being very prideful and then he said, "You sure are full of yourself aren't you." I looked at his wife's hand and said, "Yes, I am." He then looked at his wife's hand and started smiling all the way into belief. I smiled and said I love you Jesus and I love you more every day.

As I got inside the car with my little Jenny, I sat there and thought about what God had just done and I said out loud, "Jesus, you don't like melancholy do you? Jesus gives us the Joy of the Lord and Jesus gives us His strength." I smiled at my Jenny and thought "You are next little one!" My Jesus encourages and I will love Him forever! Actually, I will love Him for eternity.

ALYSSA'S FAITH AND SOWING IN THE SPIRIT.

I want to talk about Alyssa again. Isn't faith amazing? The moment Alyssa focused on Jesus and how Jesus handled the problem for Paul and Silas, she found great peace. Alyssa has great faith and her faith is in the one who will never leave her or forsake her. Her Joy and her strength are rooted deep in her love and trust in Jesus. Her court date is not for a couple weeks and she has a choice to make – either be upset for a couple weeks or walk in the peace of the one who gives peace, love and joy! We already know the path Alyssa has chosen, don't we?

The coolest thing about Alyssa's story is I have the privilege of knowing and building my faith by witnessing the faith Alyssa has in my Jesus. Iron sharpens iron, the Scripture says so. Alyssa is so special to me because of her love and trust for the Lord and how her trust can make the difference between peace in the time of trial or the turmoil of unbelief. I know for a fact the praise and worship Alyssa exhibits in her walk right now will be an example to the world around her. Every acquaintance of Alyssa is being blessed right now by watching this mighty woman of faith in our God while on her journey.

You see, Jesus said we will recognize them by their fruits. Without Jesus in our life, words can be deceiving, even our eyes can sometimes be deceiving. But when the trial of our faith in Jesus is upon us, we will shine the light of faith and love like Alyssa or we will walk in darkness and prove we don't believe by our actions. Everyone will see if we believe or not by how we handle our trial. I believe that is why Jesus said to praise Him in all things. I love the trials we are given because we have the chance to prove our belief. Trials are awesome; trials are what the world is watching for.

Let every trial be a light to the world and you will bear good fruit like Paul and Silas in the Bible story above. Read your Bible and be inspired. Read to become the Word of God, scripture says, Jesus was the word made flesh; we are flesh made into the word of God. To believe the Word is more than memorizing, more than quoting... It is actually becoming the Word and becoming is walking in faith and faith is action! Jesus said tell them the Kingdom of God is at hand. How will they know unless we live like our Savior did? So I tell you this, you can live in the kingdom of God right now! Live in the Joy of the Lord right now and give the Kingdom of God (Heaven) to all as Jesus did; right now!

One more point to make on this trial. Notice Alyssa did not call saying, "I cannot believe Jesus is letting this happen to me! I cannot figure out why or what I did wrong? I cannot figure what sin I committed to deserve this." Those thoughts are thoughts of the world and not of God. I believe thoughts like those are the thoughts of the world Jesus referred to when He said "there is a way that seems right to a man, but the end of these thoughts are death. Follow Jesus to life everlasting and enjoy a life of joy and strength on earth today.

Proverbs 14:12 There is a way that seems right to a man, but its end is the way of death.

I believe trials prove our belief or our disbelief in our loving Jesus. I believe we still hear from our Father and Jesus in the middle of our trials. And when our trial comes, all we need to do is stand firm in our belief of the love of God has for us. For God in His word says.

Ephesians 6:11 Put on the whole armor of God, that you may be able to _stand_ against the wiles of the devil.

I believe our amour is only as strong as our belief in God and our armor is our belief in how much God will protect us. We are to stand firm in our belief that Jesus lives in us and through us. He will never leave us or forsake us because Jesus loves us and has already proved His love for us. Jesus said nothing is impossible for those of us who chose to believe. Stand firm in your belief and be armored up 24/7 by simply believing God Himself is our armor.

Let us talk about David for a moment. When David said he would fight the giant, his brothers tried to protect him by giving him their armor. David refused to wear it because his faith was in his Godly armor not man made armor. Today we lock our cars, our houses, our positions and our hearts because we don't believe in God. I believe the whole armor of God is to simply believe God loves us.

Ephesians 6:10 Finally, my brethren, be strong in the Lord and in the power of His might.

I am strong in the Lord because I have faith and I believe and so I stand strong in the POWER OF HIS MIGHT! Not my might but HIS MIGHT. Anytime you fear anything; you are not standing in the power of His might.

Know that He is with you and nothing is impossible for you!

The actions of Lucifer in heaven caused Lucifer to be cast out of heaven and into hell forever. From what I understand, Lucifer never got a second chance. I thank God for His grace towards me and for Jesus given me more chances. I believe we are to praise God for our trials here on earth because if we fail our trial, we really only fail as long as we allow our selves to whaler in our failure. Thank God we have grace in our time of need. Yes, we have the grace of Jesus Christ and Father God to pick us up. Their loving grace is the (FORGIVING POWER OF GOD) please allow the love of Jesus to dust us off and start us over again. Trials are an opportunity to show our faith in our love of Jesus and our belief in Jesus to the world and by doing so we can lead others to eternal life and to the eternal love of my Jesus. Even if we fail our trial we can still win the battle by showing the world we believe in the forgiveness of God to forgive us. With God we win, win and win. Nothing is impossible for my Jesus. Think of Saul to Paul and win. Please simply ask Jesus into your heart and be transformed into an ambassador of love for Jesus.

There is only one way to succeed in the trials of life. Job succeeded in his trial because he knew without a doubt God loved him. No one could convince Job to doubt. The devil took everything physical from him, including his children. And I have been told by people who seem to know that Job knew his children were not living right by Godly standards. If this is true, it would seem in the mind of Job that he was probably thinking the devil or this trial had just put his children – his loved ones in hell. No one I know could praise God in a trial like that unless he was truly rooted in the love my God has for him and has for each one of us. Even when Job's own wife was so despondent, she told Job to curse God. The faith of Job was so strong that he didn't condemn his wife. The story of Job is a story of faith. Read it to believe it.

I want faith like that of Job and Paul and all the men from Hebrews 11. I want that same belief or faith of Job. I want the trials of Job to be in my memory so when my trials come I can be strong like Job. I believe God allows us to prove to the devil how great His creations are. And again the devil loses every time we stand firm in our belief of the love of Jesus has for us and the love of our Father has for us.

Again, how can I prove to the world that I believe if I don't have trials? Yes, I can say I will praise God in all trials of life, but I want people to see my love of Jesus in my trials of life. I love my Jesus, but knowing Jesus loves me and knowing that no one can love me more than my Jesus is the greatest revelation there is in life. And this revelation of God's love is the love that got Job through his trial, it allowed Jesus to carry the cross and His love will allow you to go through your trial and not smell like smoke. This revelation of how much God loves us – His creation is what got Jesus the man through His trial to prove to us there is no death.

Thank you Jesus for loving me! Thank You Jesus for proving your love is true every single day. I am so blessed to be loved by You! I am so blessed to know that I am loved by my Jesus. I am blessed to know there is no such thing as death. I believe the life Jesus lived in this world would have been totally impossible for any human including Jesus the man, but like He said all things are possible for those who believe in the love our Father in Heaven has for us.

I believe and I want to prove it every day by what I do and by what I say and how we, Jesus and I overcome the trials of life. I believe in the love of Jesus, the blood of the Lamb – Jesus – shed for me overcomes the devil and his trials by the word of our testimony and most importantly by not loving my own life to death. I know for a fact Jesus conquered death, so I know for a fact I will live forever. Where forever is, is up to us and what we declare now. Live in belief and be with Father God and Jesus or live in fear of going to hell and end up there.

Revelations 12:11 And they overcame him by the blood of the Lamb and by the word of their testimony, and they did not love their lives to the death.

Loving your life not unto death is simply laying down your life for the needs of others just as Jesus did. Because of this love, we can lay down our lives for other people, and change their hearts for Jesus; so they can also experience the Joy of having a relationship with Jesus. To lay down your life is only possible when you believe Jesus literally defeated death. Jesus came back from what we call death. Because of Jesus, we know life is never over. We simply step from our human shell into total spirit and eternity. Jesus gave us the choice and the privilege of deciding where our eternity is going to be spent. I pray you chose well.

152

Focus On Jesus

Okay, let us focus on Jesus. Speaking of love and my Jesus, I want to tell you a story about my Jesus and the conversation we had. One morning while talking to Jesus, I ask for an example of His love. I mean the life of Jesus is the greatest love story ever told, but I wanted to hear His example of a love story. I might have missed while reading His Word. Jesus asked me to remember the story of Mary Magdalene when she went to the tomb and found the tomb empty.

John 20:11-17 But Mary stood outside by the tomb weeping, and as she wept she stooped down and looked into the tomb. And she saw two angels in white sitting, one at the head and the other at the feet, where the body of Jesus had lain. Then they said to her, "Woman, why are you weeping?" She said to them, "Because they have taken away my Lord, and I do not know where they have laid Him." Now when she had said this, she turned around and saw Jesus standing there, and did not know it was Jesus. Jesus said to her, "Woman, why are you weeping? Whom are you seeking?" She, supposing Him to be the gardener, said to Him, "Sir, if You have carried Him away, tell me where You have laid Him, and I will take Him away." Jesus said to her, "Mary!" She turned and said to Him, "Rabboni!" (which is to say, Teacher). Jesus said to her, "Do not cling to Me, for I have not yet ascended to My Father; but go to My brethren and say to them, 'I am ascending to My Father and your Father, and to My God and your God.'"

I asked Jesus why He could not let Mary touch Him. Jesus said, "I was making a point. You see Ron, I was on my way to the biggest party heaven has ever seen." Jesus said how He had been separated from His Father for about 33 years and then gone through three days of beatings and being crucified. Then Jesus went to hell for three days, but now the big day was at hand. All Jesus needed to do was to ascend into the loving arms of our Father for the victory hug and party. While on the way to see his Father; Jesus saw Mary Magdalene crying and He stopped to comfort her.

I thought to myself how many times I did not stop when I saw someone in need because I was in a hurry. How I let my needs get in the way of helping others. Jesus, I love you and your examples are so convicting and so loving I will change and put the needs of others in front of mine as You did!

You know what is cool in the Scriptures above; Mary didn't recognize the gardener as Jesus until Jesus called Mary by her name. We are to have a personal relationship with Jesus, so personal that when Jesus calls our name we will turn around and recognize Him. I love you Jesus! Please dear Jesus help me tell others about our love affair in such a way that they want one too!

I would like to make one other little point about John 20:17. Jesus told Mary to 'go to my brethren, and say unto them, 'I ascend unto my Father and your Father and to my God and your God'. This part of Scripture is amazing to think about because it proves Jesus did not hold any unforgiveness toward His apostles. The apostles deserted Jesus six days earlier. They let Him take the beating all by Himself. Jesus went to court all by Himself. Jesus carried the cross all by Himself! I mean none of His brethren were there to support Him. Now, His friends, His chosen eleven were huddled in a locked room and as my good friend Dan pointed out to me; Jesus still calls them 'my brethren'. That is 100% forgiveness! Jesus says, "I ascend unto my Father and Your Father and my God and you're God." Jesus is telling Mary and us that we have the same Father who is His God and our God. I truly believe Jesus loves me; do you?

I hope you see the purity of the love of Jesus in the paragraphs above. Jesus is our example of the purest most perfect love of our Father God. Father God let his perfect love flow through Jesus to us and now we can flow the perfect love of Jesus to others as Jesus did. I will follow Him and let His perfect love transform me to be His forgiveness to anyone that disappoints me. I pray you will too.

Dearest Jesus, I love you and I love you more every time we talk. When we (your creation) start to realize how much we are loved by Jesus and our Father; our world will be safer, our hopes will be sky high, you will see the solution, not the problem, you will see the mountains move, you will see walking on water as an everyday occurrence and most of all you will see the loving Joy of Jesus flowing through you to transform this world and the lives of other people and your Joy of the Lord will never end!

When you know Jesus loves you and the two of you are on a first name basis, when you spend time in conversation with Jesus every day and take time to hear His voice you will never backslide. As my friend Dan says, you will *frontslide* right into the loving arms of my Jesus. Life in God is so good and yes all the time!

Gay Encounters

Trust in God is so important, yet sometimes our experiences in life seem to take us out of our trusting Him for a short time. I want to share a couple of encounters I had in the past year with gay men and a lesbian woman. When they happened I was ashamed of the encounters because I thought I listened to the wrong voice and I thought I had done something to make them happen. I tell you this: discernment is very important. My Jesus is so gentle! His corrections are so gentle. You will see what I mean as you read this. Some of this is written in the form of a letter to a girl I met named '*Every Day*' and yes that is her true name. Some of this story is written as a letter I sent to some friends.

This story will probably not be intended for new believers. It is about a lesbian lady I met at a campground whose name is *Every Day*. I believe it is powerful, but I need to tell you a part of the story that I didn't put in the letter to Every Day because I had already told her this part and I didn't want to bore her with it again. The other part of the story is her letter which you will read later.

I want to start by asking you a question: What would you do if you were in a public restroom / a shower house and while you are taking a shower a man asked you if you would give him some soap because he forgot his? As you handed him your soap you noticed he was fully aroused and in just seconds he masturbated right in front you. How would you handle that kind of situation?

Last year, I attended a Power and Love Conference in Madison, Wisconsin. After being in the church for four days and upon arriving back at the campground from church on Sunday morning, I decided to take a walk in the state park I was camping in.

The park was huge and I walked for an hour or so when I went past a man sitting in his car reading a book. He looked at me

156

and nodded *hi* as I walked by. I went down the road to the picnic area and saw the road I was walking on to be a dead end. I started walking back when I saw the same guy who said hi as I walked by his car. He was walking and nodded again so I said hi again and kept walking. Usually, I would have stopped and talked to the person passing by but I had a very uncomfortable feeling about him because he looked right at my crotch like I didn't have any clothes on.

I just kept walking and thinking how strange that was. The next thing I knew he was following me. As I walked the couple miles to the campground, I tried to lose him a couple times, but it was very obvious that he was not going away. I didn't want him to know what camper I was in so I walked over and sat on a picnic table. He walked by three or four times and then left. I thanked God he left and I thought how strange that was.

The next morning, I was hooking up my car to the motor home when he came walking by again. I couldn't believe he was back. As he walked past me, he rubbed his butt with his hand. He had those silky shorts on like basketball players wear. Then, he turned around and walked toward me again and this time as I saw him coming he rubbed himself in the privates. If that was not bad enough, he walked by a third time and rubbed his butt with both hands.

I was just about to finish hooking up the car when he sat on a picnic table. I decided to talk to him. So I walked over and said, "I think I need to apologize to you." The man looked surprised and puzzled.

I continued, "I think you want something from me, but I'm not sure what you want. So if I did something to make you think I might want to spend some time with you, I'm very sorry because I don't. I am sorry if I gave you some kind of signal that made you follow me; you see I am not sure what made you follow me yesterday or why you came back today."

I added, "And anyway, if you have some kind of itching problem going on in your private area, you should go to a doctor. The way you walk around itching yourself is nasty and if your friends saw you they might think you are weird." He looked at me like *are you real?* I said, "May God Bless you and God please heal his itching problem for him." I turned around and started walking toward my camper when he said God Bless you too. I turned back around and said, "Thank you. It was nice talking to you." He left and so did I.

I praised God that he was not as aggressive as he looked and I praised God I was leaving that area. Now, looking back I wonder if I should have tried to tell him the good news, you know Jesus loves you and Jesus wants to be in your life, not in your face. We all need relationship with my Jesus and I pray for that man to come into a relationship with God still to this day.

I have only shared this story with a couple friends. I believed I might have done something to make that man who was probably gay come on to me. After talking to Every Day, she explained that she was a lesbian and the guy's reaction to me is a game they play.

While talking to Every, I asked if she thought my shorts are too short, and could my shorts have been the signal to him. She said it was the fact I was alone and my shorts were not a signal of anything gay. She said if you think it is your shorts maybe you should wear those shorts with all the pockets (I think she called them cargo shorts). I said, "That is what he had on the night he followed me. I don't like all that weight on me and those kinds of shorts are too hot for me. Anyway, why would I want to wear the same type clothes they wear, I mean wouldn't that be a signal to them?"

I learned a lot from talking to Every Day as you will see in the letter. Now, I don't feel embarrassed anymore. My only regret comes from not talking more to these guys about Jesus. I realized when the follower man said 'God bless you' to me; I basically had an open invitation to talk to him about My Lord! I was on the way to Duluth to be part of the Go Network team and I realize I just left him sitting there. My Jesus took my guilt away by letting me know, blessing that man was all he needed me to do that day. THANK YOU JESUS! Jesus always removes guilt.

Just one more note: being with the team of the Go Network is such a blessing and I have been with the team a couple of times now. And wow, what God does through them is truly a blessing to all. Everyone knows Jesus is my best friend! Everyone on the Team of the Go Network knows Jesus on a first name basis also, and it is amazing to watch God flow through them!

I believe the man in the park received a mustard seed of God's love that day and so did I. Think what God can do with a mustard seed planted in LOVE! The possibilities are endless and the realities are yet to be seen! May God bless you and all your loved ones with mustard seeds of love and may your soil be tilled and ready to receive the seeds.

LETTER TO EVERY

Dear Every,

How is your day? How is this precious child of God?

I just want to thank you for spending time with me and hearing me with an open heart. In our conversation, you asked me to at least explore the gay options in life. I'm very sorry, but I don't think I need to explore these options to know if I would like it or not. Because I already know the kind of relationship you are talking about and it is not right for me. I believe Paul spoke quite plainly about what God thinks about the gay lifestyle in the Bible. You talked about hugs from man to man and I said that I like hugs. Jenny's hugs were so loving and special to me. I like being touched and I remember a few times in my life where someone prayed for me, I believe I received more healing from their warm touch than from their prayer. I know the prayer did more than the touch, but just a gentle warm hand on my shoulder felt great also.

I think these are positive touches, but looking for a man-to-man relationship could never achieve true love. I know Jesus loved the apostles but there is no indication at all that their love was ever sexual. So yes, I have love for my fellow men, but the love I feel toward them is a Godly love and not a sexual love. Sex is not love – it is an action. For me, love is charity and charity is a display of caring and giving and sacrificing.

Every, your life filters were very intriguing to me. I talked about some life encounters I have had lately and it was interesting to me how you viewed them as maybe some life force from somewhere was asking me to explore this type relationship. But my filter is different then yours. My filter is the Holy Spirit living inside me and the Holy Spirit of God teaching me, God's Word. I see the men and women in the gay lifestyle are very unhappy. I see them in desperate need of a loving relationship with God. The need for a relationship with God is for all people I meet. We all had childhood experiences, these experiences can dictate our future if we live in them, if we dwell in them and if we let them become our standard for how we view our life.

Most people that I meet are looking for happiness instead of a relationship with God. The man I met in the bathroom was just looking to satisfy himself or his need to have sex. A long term relationship between two males is almost never heard of, or at least I haven't heard of it. You told me that gay men see every man as someone they can have sex with. They are looking for happiness, lust, fulfillment and not Godly love and charity. Their search is for a momentary climax and not a long lasting relationship where they have to work out the details and actually give of their selves.

Another problem for me is I don't believe in happiness – rather I believe in Joyfulness. The problem I see in the gay lifestyle is they are trying to achieve joyfulness by looking for momentary happiness. Wow, I think I just described the biggest problem in the world today. I am not sure what Jesus is telling me with these encounters with gay men, but I know in due time I will find out and I believe you have been some of the answers from God for me. Thank you Every.

You see, the gay men I met are only searching for happiness. They are looking for some guy to satisfy their desire. The desire is to feed their own lust and not to give of or die of their selves. They have no joy in the lifestyle they have chosen. They are looking for happiness, not the joy of Godliness. This really is not just a gay issue. The issue of finding happiness by getting something for yourself instead of giving of yourself is a worldwide problem.

Gay men are just looking for men to fulfill their lust – they are not looking to make someone's life better or to give of themselves. This problem is not just in gay men, the problem is in straight men also. Look at how many places there are for men to go and watch the women dance naked. Men who go to places to watch girls dance naked are not there looking for a long term relationship. They believe they are only looking to get satisfied physically, but they probably have some big emotional problems they will not deal with.

For example, our government; it seems apparent by the way they govern that most of our politicians in government today do not care what is good for America. They are just trying to fulfill their own lust for power. Isn't it ironic? I am told a lot of our politicians are gay. Every, you mentioned you knew men who are married and gay. Can you imagine the confusion in their minds all the time? Their life must be like a walking hell.

I believe most people I meet are looking for something or someone to fulfill their needs. I live in campgrounds so I see people trying to find happiness in traveling or by having the biggest motor home, the biggest dog or the most dogs. Sometimes they are just running from their own children. There is a couple camping across from me now who have a nice motor home and tow vehicle. They also have a really perfect 1966 Mustang. It is plain to see he loves his mustang but she calls it a money pit. The sad fact is, so many couples I meet, seem to be at odds with each others lifestyle. It seems that in every couple there is strife; one would rather be home and not on the road, one doesn't like dogs while the other does, one says this motor home is to big, we need to down size, while the other says it is not big enough, etc.

My point is; the moment anyone looks to anything other than God to fulfill our needs, we become like waves of the sea driven by the wind and tossed in all directions. If we look to another person to fulfill our needs, we are actually setting them up to fail us. If I need you to be a certain way for me to like you and one day you don't live up to my expectation; I will not be happy. If I am not rooted in the love of Jesus, then too bad for you. I am done with you, but if I am rooted in the love of Jesus, I will protect your heart at the expense of my own.

If I need someone to be a certain way for me to have happiness, I would be in a very sad place and so vulnerable to that person. If your happiness depends on someone else being a certain way or something external to make or break your day, you have just set that person up to fail you and you have just given that person power over your happiness.

I cannot even think how sad it is for a person to hang out in a bathroom looking for some kind of experience to bring happiness into his life. That lifestyle is sadness to the max and it will only lead you right into depression. Like the depression in the couples in the paragraph above, they are covering their hurt hearts by looking for something other than the Joy of the Lord to make them happy.

Our identity, our happiness, our love for fellow men simply cannot be derived from someone else, something material, or from an achievement of our own. Our identity is not in how many people love us or for some even, if we have a ministry or not. Our identity is not in the things of this world. I will not be held down by the things of the world. My identity is in my relationship with my Jesus. I know for a fact that Jesus loves me! I mean, Jesus sees something so special in me. Jesus went to the cross so I might believe and live in relationship with Him.

When I meet people, I am not trying to make them like me or love me because I know Jesus loves me. My goal in life is not to get something from others, but rather my goal is to give the love of Jesus to others. I want others to experience the love of Jesus so they can have Heaven on earth. I like it when people tell me that they love me. But if I need them to tell me they love me, I am actually trying to have them fill a void in my life. A life modeled after Jesus is a life full of giving and giving is joyfully fulfilling. Jesus said He came to set us free of the bondage of this world. Because I have heard the Word of God and let the word of God in my heart, I don't need any physical relationship to make my day. I have my identity, I am a Son of God, and I rejoice in His love for me.

To know our true identity we need to study the life of Jesus. True identity will come when we realize Jesus brings joy into your life and Jesus is the source of all good in this life. It is so simple to me. I believe the people I meet in life are not just accidents. I believe I have something to share with them and if they understand or come into even a little understanding, like a mustard seed of the love of Jesus, then I have great joy. If they don't understand me then I know for a fact that God will send them another messenger who will get a chance to speak to their heart. Do you see the freedom in that? I am not burdened by the problems of the world

– I am not here to transform the world as a whole, but because I know I am loved by Jesus and with Jesus in me I can transform the world one heart at a time.

Every, I enjoyed our talks. I realized how much insight I learned about the gay lifestyle. I mean, when the man was masturbating right in front of me he asked me, "Are you going to hit me?" I did not understand his question at all. Now, thanks to you I do. At the time I thought I had sent him some kind of message of hate or disdain for what he was doing and hate and disdain will never transform anyone's heart and it is not the love of Jesus. I didn't like him masturbating in front of me, but I didn't want to do the work of the devil and tell him something stupid like you're going to hell, so get away from me. Now I know from your insight that he sees himself as hated, different and even some Christians will hit him for doing the things he is doing.

When Jesus went into the tax collectors house, Jesus didn't tell the tax collector what he needed to do to change his life. Jesus didn't give him a list of sins. Jesus never told him to first repent of these sins and then they can talk. Jesus just lets His love flow into the man and the man wanted the joy of Jesus. The man repented for ripping off his own people, he promised to reform and to repay the people he had ripped off. The man received the Joy of the Lord from Jesus into his heart and for his commitment to repent he received the forgiveness of the Lord. There is no better gift you can give than to set the captives free.

I am glad I did not reject that man out of the bathroom because that would have just reinforced the idea that Christians are condemning people and Christians only love the loveable people. I know for a fact Jesus never condemned anyone for their sin, but Jesus asked them to believe in Him and to believe in the love of Jesus, for Jesus said, "It is the goodness of God that will lead a man to repentance."

I could cry for that gay man, and for the men trapped in that lifestyle. I cannot even think of a life so useless. I mean, to hang out in a bathroom night after night, hoping someone will come in and do whatever they do to please each other; it is pretty much unthinkable to me. I thank God for trusting me and for putting me

163

in this situation so we, Jesus and I, could demonstrate the love of my Jesus to that man.

I think about that night and I think if the tub in my camper had not cracked and started leaking I would have taken my shower in my own camper, like usual. My only regret is I didn't tell that man the good news about Jesus but I believe I did give him a small dose of the love of Jesus by my answer to his question, "Are you going to hit me?" I realize now by the look on his face that he was surprised by my answer when I replied, "Why would I hit you?" Within seconds he was finished, he dressed and left as fast as he could. I thought to myself, "I should have talked to him about the Lord, but I was showering and so that made me uncomfortable. I had just seen a man masturbate and that made me uncomfortable. I now know what he was thinking when he asked that question and I will be bolder and I will talk about the love of Jesus if an occasion like that ever comes up again. Thanks to your insight.

My Jesus is so amazing! I didn't talk to that man or tell him I was a Christian. I know my reaction to his question puzzled him. I stayed in that campground a couple more days and I saw him drive by my camper as I was cooking dinner out on the picnic table. My camper has a big bumper sticker on it that says '*CoffeeTimeWith Jesus.com*'. It is six-feet wide and twelve inches high, you cannot miss it. Even though I didn't talk to him about being a Christian, he knows I am by my reaction to him and by my bumper sticker. Thank you Jesus! I pray he goes to my website and reads the teachings there.

As I am writing this, I remembered the conversation I had with a man that I met in Texas. He was a great teacher of the Word. Without any prompting on my part, he told a story. He was down on his luck for a while, he was living in his car and he went to a YMCA to shower and clean up every night. He described the shower there as one big room with twelve showerheads. He led some man to the Lord and to be baptized while both were taking a shower. The reason for him telling me that story that night was not clear to me until now.

The night the gay man ask me for some soap, I missed a golden opportunity to share the good news in the shower that night because I was ashamed to share the good news while I was naked.

So today, I ask my source Jesus if He had ever preached naked. I asked because I know we should only do what we seen the Father do and sense Jesus was His Father's ambassador while here on earth, we should do as Jesus did. Jesus answered me, He said read what I did at the last supper.

John 13:4-5 (Jesus) Rose from supper and laid aside His garments, took a towel and girded Himself. 5 After that, He poured water into a basin and began to wash the disciples' feet, and to wipe them with the towel with which He was girded.

I believe Jesus on a number of occasions was either naked or scantily dressed and it did not stop Him from preaching the good news, so from now on it will not stop me, even if I am naked and even if I am nailed to a cross.

Jesus in his Word and in everything he taught us, told us "what we focus on is what we become"

Matthew 6:21 For where your treasure is, there your heart will be also.

If your treasure is finding an experience in a bathroom, then that is where your focus is. While you are looking and focusing on the experience, with little or no regard for the other person and your whole purpose in life is to satisfy your own selfish desires then that is where your heart is. Your heart is focused on yourself and not being the love of Jesus.

You see if I focus on my own needs or if I need someone to fill my needs then my focus is on me and what I need. Self-centered life is a life of no joy because even if I meet someone that filled every one of my desires today, chances are they will not be able to fill every need I have tomorrow or next week. So the search goes on and you will never be fulfilled.

The gay lifestyle is so unnatural to me. I mean, that man sat on a toilet hoping someone would come into the shower house so

165

he could be fulfilled some way. If that man put that same effort and time into knowing Jesus, he would find the Joy of the Lord would overtake him. His needs would be met with an everlasting love from my Jesus. His desire for love would be satisfied. He would wake up excited about the day and not be thinking or hoping someone would walk into a shower house that would excite him into momentary happiness.

Every, you told me how public bathrooms are like open doors or safe havens for the gay lifestyle. Knowing these men hang out in bathrooms, is just so sad. I thought, for most people's bathrooms are a place to poop or to pee. I just cannot think of getting up in the morning and thinking, "I'm going to hang out in a public bathroom all day and try not to look gay."

Love is so powerful when love is centered on the life of Jesus and what Jesus wants done today. I know I respected my Jenny so much in life because she never focused on herself. She was a stay-at-home mom and I have never been a really big provider. Although I did provide a nice house for Jenny, it was Jenny who made the house a home. She watched our children and the neighbor's children a lot. She delighted in being there when these children needed her. I look back on her life and realize how her whole life was about giving and never receiving. I believe it was her Christ-like life that made Jenny so special to me and so loveable to me.

I can tell you that Jenny and our life together were never about sex. We never once had sex. We did make love though. I hear married people talk about how many times they have sex and I think and I wonder how many times they make love.

I think that is why the needs of all human relationships fail or fall short at some point. I know some people find divorce easier than trying to work things out. Life is amazing to me. I have seen people get married and on the wedding day I thought this is a marriage made in heaven because they seemed so happy only to find out latter they were getting divorced.

I find in my walk with my Jesus the more I focus on my Jesus and what he needs done today the more joyful my life becomes. It is so simple and so rewarding. I looked back on the night when I walked into the shower house and the lights came on from a motion sensor. As I walked to the shower area, I had to walk past the sinks, the urinals and the toilets. There was a man sitting on the toilet with the toilet stall door open. I was surprised and startled by him being there because the lights were off when I walked in the bathroom, shower house. He told me he was having a bowel problem and he had sat there so long the lights went off.

I walked to the last shower, but there was no individual dressing room, just a long bench to put you're your clothes on. He came back to my shower and asked to borrow some soap, saying he forgot his. The shower curtain was partly missing and ripped so I guess he was able to see me taking a shower. As you know, he was so aroused he masturbated right in front of me. I realize now I was in shock and I let the fact I was naked stop me from talking about the Lord to him. If only I had focused on my Jesus instead of the situation, I could have and should have told him the good news about my Jesus. I will not let circumstances stop me again. My focus has to be and will always be on building the kingdom of God even in a public bathroom.

I really couldn't figure out why I told you some of the circumstances of my life. I asked Jesus about the night I met you. Now I know I needed to talk with someone with an understanding heart, and someone that would not be judgmental. I think most Christians would think I handled that situation all wrong and should have just left the moment I saw him sitting on the toilet. From talking to you, I have learned a lot and I thank you for your time and understanding. I pray for my Jesus to raise someone up to tell that man the good news of my Jesus.

I want to say when that man came out of the toilet stall and looked at me; I felt a strong desire to leave. I know in my mind I wanted to get out of there fast, but I just turned and got into the shower stall real fast. Now I know the reason I stayed was I also felt a prompting from the Lord in my heart to stay.

When the man left the bath house I felt I let the Lord down, I actually felt dirty, but I know feelings of guilt are not of a God. Guilt is how the devil separates us from God. Now I believe I did help that man by simply not rejecting him as weird or offensive. Plus, I now know him and can pray for him to come to know the

Lord and to experience the Joy of the Lord. Jesus in His word never rejected anyone nor did He call them sinners. The people rejected Jesus and His love so they could continue to sin.

After talking to you and now having some of your insight, I think God had me handle the situation correctly. I mean if I had condemned him by telling him to get out, or said I'm calling the cops or if I had hit him, in his mind I would have been reinforcing the fact that he is hated and weird. He would know that Christians talk about love, but put someone in their path that is living outside the morals of Christian beliefs and they condemn him. I know in my mind he needs to know the reason Jesus came was to model the love of His Father to us. The love of Jesus will transform him, but running him off or hitting him, would only make his situation worse.

Another choice you talked about would have been for me to participate with him. In doing so, I would be condoning his actions and telling him that it is okay. I think you might have been thinking that if you want to show him love, you should participate with him. I believe what he wanted and desired is sex, not love. It would be coming into agreement with his desire for sex and I would have been feeding his desire for what Jesus called unnatural. So to me that was never a viable choice.

I know there are people that seem to be born gay right from birth. I really don't need to nor will I try to explain the reason for that, but I do need to be part of the solution. For me, the solution is simply demonstrating the love of Jesus to them and letting God be God and letting God be the judge and letting God bring the increase of saved souls.

When you told me how I should try having sex with a man just to see if I would like it or if it would feel right to me. You said nothing bad would come from trying it. You also assured me and even reassured me of that fact! The reasons you gave made sense to a natural person grounded in natural facts. The coolest part of being loved by Jesus is He will lead you into true truth. When I asked Jesus about the things we discussed, Jesus said, "Read Proverbs 24" while we were talking and having my Coffee Time together.

The first verse is the right answer and Jesus gave it to me:

Proverbs 24:1 Do not be envious of evil men, nor desire to be with them

Read all of Proverbs 24 and you will hear Jesus talking to you also. Yes, I had some crazy events happened in my life, but my life is not determined by events. My joy and my identity come from knowing that I am made in the image and likeness of the one who created me. I am His ambassador here on earth. I am to preach the Word of God to everyone, everywhere and every day. I know now I am to teach His Word no matter what the circumstances are. I believe these circumstances include meeting you, because you have given me insight into the gay lifestyle. Jesus used that insight to give me new strength in my relationship to my loving Jesus and to let the love of Jesus flow through me to others, even in a bathroom.

I know Jesus loves me and I walk in that revelation. I know it is Jesus who defines who I am and so if I ever find myself in a similar situation like that again, I will preach the Word boldly and lovingly to all. I will not condemn anyone because Jesus never condemned. I will be a loving example of the love of Jesus to all because Jesus showed us how it is His loving Goodness that will led a man to repentance and not our condemnation of their lifestyle.

You know, for a lot of people, repentance is a work and something they are dreading to think of. For me, repentance is a gift of freedom that you receive when you open your heart to the love of my Jesus.

I believe that we are all on this earth with a purpose. I know some of us have discerned the voices we hear and know who is talking to us. I believe when we discern and when we know we are hearing from the Lord, Jesus will be able to use us in any circumstance. I believe that is why we are here. I believe we are here to be the ambassadors for Jesus in all circumstances.

I am surrendered to my Jesus and I know Jesus will use me for His good and that is the Joy of the Lord in my heart. The joy of the Lord sure beats being depressed and wasting your life sitting in a bathroom, being in need of something or someone to fulfill me or bring happiness into my life which is a life of disappointment. Yes for a couple months I wasn't able to figure out the meaning of that night, but now Jesus explained it and he used you, thank you!

I think about meeting you and after talking for quite some time, how you saw the need to tell me you are gay. I pray you felt the need to tell me because you did not see any judgment in me. I know you have a relationship with Jesus and my prayer for you is the same prayer I pray for myself – to come into a deeper loving relationship with my Jesus. I know I am loved and so I can love! Jesus gives my life direction, usefulness, meaning, and the most powerful gift of all – Jesus gives me the ability to love others. Jesus you are so good to me, my only hope is to be a Godly inspiration to others and to continually grow in my relationship with my Jesus. I love my Jesus, but more than my love for Him I know Jesus loves me. No one can love you more than my Jesus!

Someday, our paths might cross again and I look forward to that day 'Every Day'.

Remember, you are a precious child of God! NEVER FORGET THAT!

The love of Jesus is an everlasting love of joy and not momentary happiness like the pleasures of this world. In closing, I would like to tell you a short story about another man I met. After talking about God for a couple days he asked me what God thinks of gay men and lesbian women. I told him the Bible is very clear where God stands on this issue. God in His word says;

Romans 1:24-28 Therefore God also gave them up to uncleanness, in the lusts of their hearts, to dishonor their bodies among themselves, who exchanged the truth of God for the lie, and worshiped and served the creature rather than the Creator, who is blessed forever. Amen. For this reason God gave them up to vile passions. For even their women exchanged the natural use for what is against nature. Likewise also the men, leaving the natural use of the woman, burned in their lust for one another, men with men committing what is shameful, and receiving in themselves the penalty of their error which was due. And even as they did not like to retain God in their knowledge, God gave them over to a debased mind, to do those things which are not fitting

As you can see, God has a lot to say about this subject. Please read all of Romans 1 and you will see Jesus never told us to judge. We can recognize sinners and we are to change their hearts by demonstrating the love of Jesus to them. Jesus even warned us about judging.

Romans 2:1-4 Therefore you are inexcusable, O man, whoever you are who judge, **for in whatever you judge another you condemn yourself;** for you who judge practice the same things. But we know that the judgment of God is according to truth against those who practice such things. And do you think this, O man, you who judge those practicing such things, and doing the same, that you will escape the judgment of God? Or do you despise the riches of His goodness, forbearance, and longsuffering, not knowing that the goodness of God leads you to repentance?

Upon reading these Scriptures, you will see God never once told us to Judge. It is God who will judge us! Jesus actually commanded us not to judge. We are only told to recognize sinners as Jesus recognized them and we are told to love them as Jesus loved them. How could we possibly expect to change someone's lifestyle by condemning them, hitting them, calling them names, or telling them to get away from us? Those are all tactics of the devil! I am an ambassador of Jesus! The devil has enough people helping him spread his hatred, I refuse to help the devil spread is hatred.

Jesus told us who He came for, and I believe we are here for the same reason.

Mark 2:17 When Jesus heard *it*, He said to them, "Those who are well have no need of a physician, but those who are sick. I did not come to call t*h*e righteous, but sinners, to repentance.

I believe Jesus when He himself said:

Matthew 18:14 Even so it is not the will of your Father who is in heaven that one of these little ones should perish.

You see, our job is to teach FROM the love of our Father and our Brother in Heaven. We teach FROM His love not OF His love! We can only teach FROM His love if we know we are loved. Knowing we are loved by God will enable us to love others by giving from His love in us. If you only know of His love and haven't experienced the love of God, you will never have anything to give. We have to know in our hearts that without a doubt, we are the little one that our Father is talking about when Jesus said

Matthew 18:14 Even so it is not the will of your Father who is in heaven that one of these little ones should perish.

I wake up excited every day to see how God is going to use me today. I never thought that I would end up in those circumstances, but I believe in Jesus when He said it is the will of the Father that not even one of our brothers or sisters should perish. Jesus is our example and Jesus went right into the sinner's house and had dinner with them and through the love He showed them He converted them. I believe Jesus when he said it is the goodness of Jesus that will lead a man to repentance. I believe I am protected by my Jesus and so I have no fear about going anywhere.

Realize judgment comes after death so we are given all our entire life to seek Him! Our job is to help restore the lost sheep and not to destroy the lost sheep by condemning them. The devil condemns us and he doesn't need our help, to spread his wickedness. We are to be an ambassador for Jesus not a condemning ambassador of the devil.

We do not need to condone sinners of any kind because Jesus never condoned the sinner. He simply showed us there is a better way to convert – a way filled with Joy and usefulness, a way filled with purpose and there is a reward for our service called Heaven. We can have Heaven now, right here on earth and share heaven with everyone, just as Jesus did while here on earth.

The man who asked me, "What does Jesus think about gays?" also talked a little about guns and defending himself. I asked him to please read *Freedom from Self in the Joy of the Lord* book. I see the protection of my loving Jesus in my life everywhere, every day and I believe carrying a gun would truly say I don't believe you, Jesus. Smith Wigglesworth once said, "I would rather die believing then live doubting!"

The more you know Jesus the more you will realize is love for you is real!

One more thought, before Every Day left, she told me, "Ron you are a writer and you need to write these stories down!" I thought to myself, they are too embarrassing. After talking to my Jesus, I realized they were written down in my heavenly book of life. Also, writing my life down on paper is good for me and I know that is how God makes sense of things to me. So thank you again *Every*! It was good advice and God used this letter, His writing to take away my embarrassment. Thank you Jesus, I love you too!

I have now shared this story with a couple people and they were blessed and transformed by this story! GOD IS SO GOOD!!!

Jenny, Ron and Jesus love you!

Reactions to My Letter to Every

I have had some pretty interesting reactions to this letter. One lady that I met at a campground called and told me how this letter opened her heart. She told me about her daughter, who takes pictures of weddings professionally as her way of making a living. Her daughter was wondering how to handle a situation she had gotten into.

Recently her daughter had received a phone call request to do a wedding on a certain date. After checking the date, she told the man the date was open and she would do the wedding. The man was really happy that she said yes since she has an excellent reputation for capturing the love of the couple on film. Later she found out the man who called was gay and was marrying a gay man.

First of all, I believe there can never – I mean never be an actual wedding of any gay people. For me a wedding has to be blessed by God to be valid. No justice of the piece can perform a true wedding – all they have is the power to do is a contract. They even say, *"By the power vested in me by the State (whatever state they are in) I pronounce you man and wife."* Do you see the words the State give them power to perform contracts not weddings? There is a file somewhere with a contract in it. They can give you a legal contract, but not a wedding. I will call this situation a contract not a wedding.

So here's the dilemma: she told her mother she didn't know what to do. Men marrying men are against her morals. She wanted to tell the man this is against her morals and for this reason she would not do the wedding. She also knew if she told the man she doesn't do gay weddings or contracts, she could be sued and she had heard of people losing the court battle and losing their home and their business in the process.

Her mother realized after reading the letter about the gay men I had encountered that her daughter had a great opportunity to witness to these gay men and she could be an ambassador for Jesus by living the love of Jesus Christ to these men. I pray her daughter will trust Jesus is living in her and have faith that Jesus will give her words to say to these men, words that will touch the hearts of these men. We are called to be an example of the love of Jesus. It is the goodness of Jesus that will lead a man to repentance. Now, will these men see the goodness of God, if we, His ambassadors don't show them the love of Jesus? Trust in God and know in your heart Jesus will put words in your heart that will impact all men forever.

I believe Jesus is living in her daughter and Jesus through her daughter will impact these men's lives forever. Jesus is true love. True love is charity. Charity is giving, caring and sacrifice. Following Jesus is more than singing in church on Sunday – it is dying to yourself and picking up your cross every day. When these men witness what true love is first hand in the life of her daughter as she plants mustard seeds of the love of Jesus in them, their life, their hopes, their dreams and their hearts will be transformed into a life of Joy for the Lord. There will probably be a lot of people at the reception, so the opportunity to spread Jesus seeds of love is unlimited. One mustard seed, sowed in the love of Jesus will transform some ones heart.

I was taught by my parents as a child that one bad apple will spoil the whole batch. Now I am taught by Jesus that one good seed of love will transform the hearts of many. I believe in Jesus, *do you?*

I pray for guidance for the photographer and for her to refresh her mind with the Romans chapters of the Bible. I pray she hears form Jesus because Jesus will be her path and Jesus will strengthen her. Jesus will also lead her to look at the Scriptures to show her how Jesus would handle this. I pray she knows Jesus is her best friend for Jesus said, "I will never leave you or forsake you." This one verse is enough to make me want Jesus as my best friend. She will need this reassurance at the contract and the reception.

I hear your question; didn't Jesus send his apostles out two by two; therefore shouldn't she take someone with her? You know what, she is taking someone with her – she has Jesus in her heart and from the heart she will speak the words of Jesus. This is so simple to me; it is not a yes and no question. It is simply an opportunity to be an ambassador for Jesus. Jesus has more faith in us than we do with ourselves sometimes. Jesus sent the apostles out two by two because they had not been born again and had not received the Holy Spirit yet. I know she is up to this challenge because Jesus said He would not give us more then we can handle.

After discussing this situation over with some friends, they respectfully disagreed with me. They asked, "Can you imagine Jesus taking pictures of a gay wedding?" I said, "No, but I cannot picture Jesus going into a known sinner's house either, but He did." They also stated if the photographer does her job, she would be condoning the gay contract. For me, condoning the gay lifestyle would sound like this – it's okay you believe what you want and I will believe what I want, have a nice day. In my mind, I do not see this as condoning a marriage between two men. I see it as an opportunity to spread the word of God to people who might not listen under other circumstances.

I know for a fact that God doesn't want for any of His creation to perish; Jesus says so in His Word. I know if she decides not to do the contract, God will raise someone else up to give them a chance to repent. The salvation of these men doesn't depend on her taking or not taking pictures of the contract. I believe God will raise someone else up to shine the love of Jesus into their life if she decides not to do their contract.

What if she doesn't do the contract because she is afraid of being sued, wouldn't that be fear? We cannot let fear dictate our lives. Fear is faith in the devil and fear only brings turmoil and worry. Jesus said that His perfect love cast out fear. What if she does the contract thinking their salvation depends on her? She would be doing it out of guilt and guilt is not a motivation of God. The devil will use guilt to bring on shame and more 'what if' questions: *What if he sues me? What if I lose in court? What if we lose our home where will we live?*

For those what if questions, I say, what if she decides to do the contract to show these men the love of Jesus? What if the perfect love of Jesus flows through her and transforms someone's heart. When the contract is over she will rest and be in peace knowing the seeds of God's love have been planted and she will rest by letting God bring the increase.

What if she knows God dwells inside her? Fear, worry and turmoil will be back in hell where they belong and she will rest knowing the perfect love of Jesus has been released on the earth. Jesus already defeated the devil and all that He asks of us is to believe it! What if we look at the possibilities and what if Jesus can put a check mark in the Jesus column simply because we are willing vessels of His love? What if Jesus wins someone's heart because we allowed Him to flow through us even at a gay contract?

THE VOICE OF GOD

The first requirement to do the will of God is to recognize the voice of God. You see, it will be very difficult to have a close relationship with God if God cannot talk to you plainly. Faith in someone you do not correspond with will not grow. To love a God you never heard from would be as impersonal as to say I love a tree.

I mean, you could hug a tree and set in the shade of the tree and enjoy the benefits of the tree – you could even talk to the tree, sing to the tree, wave flags at the tree, but the tree could never hug you back or tell you how much it loves you. Some people even give the wood of the tree credit for things going right in their life. You probably heard people do it too when they say, "Knock on wood we had a safe trip!" or "Knock on wood the car ran good." Do you think they are hearing from God?

Do you think the same people who give credit to wood, will call on a tree if the doctor said they have cancer. Do you think they should go tell the tree, "I have cancer. Oh tree, please help me. I'll give you the credit if you do help me great tree." These tree lovers will tell everyone to knock on wood if they want something good. The problem is there are people believing them because they start knocking on wood. To a believer in God, that sounds crazy! And saying, knock on wood the weather is good; well I believe in God so when I hear people giving credit to wood; I think, PLEASE GOD give me your words of love to help them. Let us give the credit to God for it is God who is the giver of all good gifts. Worshiping trees really is as stupid as worshiping mother earth or living an alternative gay lifestyle trying to be happy. I know for a fact none of these people living that way are discerning the voice of God.

My point is this. To God which sin is bigger? We know what Jesus said about homosexuals and you might be thinking I'm not gay, so I am safe; I just like to hug trees or I just want to protect mother earth and Jesus wants us to protect mother earth, doesn't he? I am a good person I love my dog and if I was in that bathroom that night I would of ran out of there. The gay life style is more intrusive into our life and more in our face then tree hugging, but they are both the sin of none belief.

Gays marring gays; lesbians marring lesbians or sitting in a bathroom hoping someone will come in and get crazy with you is like thanking wood the weather is good or trying to please mother earth. These people have either never heard of God or God has been misrepresented to them. Either way we Christians are the ambassadors of Jesus and as such we are the solution if we are not afraid to speak boldly of His love He has for all of us everywhere.

Most Christians I know probably would not even have a problem with someone knocking on wood. Whether or not to take pictures of a gay contract is a mater of discerning the voice of God. Whether or not to give credit to wood because the weather is good is a mater of discerning the voice of God. Christians need to discern the voice of God to help the lost sheep; you see we all need discernment. Discerning the voice of God is the only way we will transform hearts to the Lord. Remember we Christians do not judge but we recognize the need for God in others by there life style. We recognize the sin of unbelief in the gay life style and the sinners should see and recognize the goodness of God in us. Please read discernment in the Joy of the Lord book. If you need one call and I will send you one free. 513 377 1727

I hope you see we Christians need to be out in the world, we need to shin the light of God where ever we go; bathrooms, gay weddings, or to people giving wood credit for something good. We

178

need to discern the voice of God and we will discern by being familiar with His word by being in His word.

Our missionary work is the person standing next to you. If the person next to you is gay or hugging a tree; please gently love them back into the light, love and Joy of Jesus Christ. To me the word of God is so clear; love the Lord with all your heart and all your soul and all your mind. Jesus is the judge; our focus is on the Lord and our purpose is to be a vessel of love to ALL. Jesus plainly told us where our joy comes from! Go boldly and proclaim His word to someone for the Joy of the Lord is only as contagious as we make it.

Have you ever wondered what Jesus would have said if one of the apostles answered Him "I will come with you in a couple months, right now I need to keep fishing because I am trying to raise $4000.00 dollars to go on a two week mission trip to Africa." Truthfully I don't ponder that question or how Jesus would answer it. I have God living in me so I have everything I need to be a missionary and a vessel of His love to everyone today and everyday. I have a pretty simple life because I have the faith of a child and I know God loves me.

THE BEST GIFTS

To experience the best gift from God – His loving personal relationship, all we need to do is open our heart when we hear God say, "Come follow Me." God is asking us to come follow Him 24/7. We open our heart by simply saying, "Dear Jesus, I want to know you intimately." Yes! Ask God into your heart right now and God will reveal how much He loves you and misses you. How much God loves you is revealed in His word. Quietly read His word and you will be hearing His voice. Hearing from God is joy beyond our understanding. Knocking on wood will eventually hurt your hand and bring on a devil of no understanding, no love, and no hope. Can you imagine seeing someone in a wheel chair and telling them *have a nice day and I will go huge ten trees for you.*

Jesus in His word said faith comes by hearing and hearing by the word of God.

Romans 10:17 So then faith comes by hearing, and hearing by the word of God.

We need to hear the Word of God so we can have faith in God. We will hear God's voice when we read His Word quietly and allow the voice of Jesus through His word into our heart.

Hebrews 11:6 But without faith *it* is impossible to please *Him*, for he who comes to God must believe that He is, and *that* He is a rewarder of those who diligently seek Him.

To diligently seek God, we must first recognize His voice. To diligently seek God, simply read His word – simply listen for His voice as you read and simply believe Him. For me, simple belief in God is believing His Word without any other proof. Scientists may prove the Word true and I don't care because I already believed it. Scientists may have evidence that the Word of God is false and I could cry for those scientists for they are lost trying to find truth in their own strength. I will not be swayed by their findings, for I will forever believe God's Word anyway. All my faith is in the word of God weather I understand it or not. When we diligently seek a relationship with God, God will reward us with peace Joy and most of all His love. Try to get that from a scientific finding, a tree or mother earth.

John 10:5 Yet they will by no means follow a stranger, but will flee from him, for they do not know the voice of strangers.

Could a stranger's voice be the latest scientific finding? Ask God for discernment and you will have it. The devil will flee and take his strange voice with him. The perfect love of Jesus is in the perfect voice of Jesus who wants to live in your perfected God filled heart for Jesus. Please welcome Jesus in and fear of everything such as gay contracts will flee.

Genesis 1:26 Then God said, "Let Us make man in Our image, according to Our likeness; let them have dominion over the fish of the sea, over the birds of the air, and over the cattle, over all the earth and over every creeping thing that creeps on the earth."

We are made to be the image and likeness of God. The devil tries every day to form us in his image and likeness which is SIN. Jesus came and restored us to His image and likeness LOVE. THANK YOU JESUS!!! I simply believe and I am rewarded with His Loving spirit inside me. Notice we have dominion over everything on earth except other human beings. We do not transform hearts by commanding them to change or by hiding behind morals. We simply let the goodness of God loose on the earth by being the ambassadors for the Goodness of Jesus – doing so will transform us into ambassadors Jesus asked us to be. You want the best gift simply be an ambassador of God.

Love is a gift from God. I believe the love of God is the reward for diligently seeking Him. I believe we can walk in His love and flow the love of Jesus to all. Simply through faith, Jesus is with you and Jesus lives inside of you. He will make the impossible become possible. If you recognize the voice of God, a stranger's voice you will not follow. Jesus says these truths in His Word. Read the word of God and you will see the life of Jesus as our example to follow. Anything we do from fear, in fear or because of fear is following the stranger's voice.

Jesus is not just some distant being waiting to call you home in something called the *rapture*. We have some work to do; we are here to build the Kingdom of God by simply walking in His love. We have a purpose and our purpose is transforming the world, one heart at a time. We are called to be teachers of the Word of God through our actions and by our words and by the guidance of the Holy Spirit. The Holy Spirit lives in me by Faith and He has all the gifts.

If you have the realization of who you are in Jesus and if you come to believe you are a child of God made in His image and likeness, this revelation will enable you can walk right into the house of a sinner and transform them like Jesus did to Zacchaeus. If you are not rooted in His perfect love then you should not do the contract even if you think you are pleasing God by doing it. Trying to please God to show Him we love Him is backwards. I mean, if the photographer takes pictures of the contract because she is in fear of losing everything or because she is trying to please God, she will only be operating in worldly works and not the kingdom of God. The only works that please God are works of faith. She will need faith to know while she is there taking the pictures she is actually there to spread the love of Jesus and by faith she will know the love of Jesus is flowing through her. Giving the kingdom of God is giving the love of God. By faith we know God tells us where to go and what to say:

Matthew 10:6-8 But go rather to the lost sheep of the house of Israel. And as you go, preach, saying, 'The kingdom of heaven is at hand.' Heal the sick, cleanse the lepers, raise the dead, cast out demons. Freely you have received, freely give.

In this Scripture, we see the need to go to the lost sheep. For me, the men and women of the gay lifestyle are just some of the lost sheep and we need to tell everyone the Kingdom of heaven is at hand! The Kingdom of heaven is not just the go to goal – it is at hand. Then Jesus tells what the kingdom of God is here on earth. Jesus shows us how to prove what we believe and how to demonstrate our belief when Jesus said:

Matthew 10:8 Heal the sick, cleanse the lepers, raise the dead, cast out demons. Freely you have received, freely give.

Remember, it is the goodness of God that will lead a man to repentance and not your goodness, but the goodness of God flowing through you. Remember, we do not judge – Jesus is the judge for He sits on the judgment seat. We can and will recognize there is a need for the love of God in someone and we can be the vessel of His love if we choose to be. You know, you received your heart transformation free from God so freely give transformations by being the love of Jesus to all. Allowing Jesus to love you will allow the love of Jesus to flow through you and you will see heart transformations everywhere you go. You will see the love of Jesus flow and you will see people thanking God instead of knocking on wood, you will see the joy of the Lord established in the kingdom of God again.

If we try to spread the Kingdom of God in our own strength, we will only burn ourselves out. If our motivation is to show Jesus we trust in Him or to show Jesus we are not in fear or to prove we love Him, those motivations will prove we are working in our own strength and we might be very disappointed if no one is transformed. We will be trying to show Jesus our love for Him by trying to make a transformation happen. Christians who work in their own strength trying to please God will probably backslide at some point, or become what we call *burnt out*. Transformations happen when we let the love of Jesus flow through us.

However, when Christians truly ask God into their heart, their life will begin to transform. Jesus called it a renewing of the mind. Our job as Christians is to set the desire for others to be transformed by being the light and the joy of the Lord to others. Have you ever heard a preacher say, "I'm so excited" and you have a hard time staying awake during the message. True excitement is contagious and is transferred to others by your excitement not your talk. Like a comedian doesn't open his show by telling you he is funny, he just starts making you laugh and then you tell him you were so funny tonight. True joy is contagious when demonstrated and not just talked about. We are to give a desire to be transformed and then we step back and let God transform their hearts.

Jesus said for us to let our light shine to ALL men. Think of it this way: If you walk into a dark room (a gay wedding) and someone turns on a bright light, (the perfect love of Jesus) everyone will know who the light is and the light is on because they will see your light shining. By allowing our life to become transparent, our light (our life) will be shining before ALL men.

Our light will be brilliant when we plug into the power source of Jesus. All light has a power source. When you plug a light into a live power source, the light will shine. We need to know Jesus is our power source and His power is in us and His love is for us. If we try to be the source we will burn out. Our power source is Jesus and our power is in knowing He loves us. Jesus said His perfect love cast out fear. We will not fear dark places (gay weddings) when we know Jesus lives in side us and loves through us. We will not fear! We will shine brilliantly and transparently to ALL without fear. Perfect love is fearless; Jesus said so! Believe it!

I believe sometimes we hide our light under the bushel basket of morals. Sometimes we hide behind our morals and expect man's justice system to up hold our morals. Hiding in the court system and expecting the courts to shine our morals for us is likened to singing in church every Sunday about how great our God is and five minutes later we are broken standing in a prayer line for prayer, or arguing with our spouse about where we are going to eat. I mean, do we believe what we sing, do we have our faith in God or the person praying. Do we have our faith in the court system and expect them to uphold our morals? Jesus said let your light so shine before ALL men. Jesus didn't say go to court and hope they up hold your morals so you can keep your light shining. We need to remember we have the strength of God in us, we don't hide our love for God, we manifest it by living it.

> **2Co 4:1-2** Therefore, since we have this ministry, as we have received mercy, **we do not lose heart.** You see we have a ministry of mercy not judgment for what we meet out or sow is what we will receive. Jesus says even if you don't see results of your mercy towards others "WE DO NOT LOSE HEART." But we have renounced the hidden things of shame, not walking in craftiness nor handling the word of God deceitfully, but by manifestation of the truth commending ourselves to every man's conscience in the sight of God.

We do not come into agreement with the hidden things of shame (SIN) or walk in the love of God in church and be deceitful in our dealings all week long like watching dirty movies at home. Here we see we are to live as manifestations of the truth of God by living the Godly love of Jesus to everyman's conscience. For we are in the sight of our loving God 24/7 If we hide our beliefs in the courts, we are hidden to the lost sheep such as those in gay lifestyle. We are not to go to court to uphold our beliefs we are commanded to live our beliefs by manifestation of the truth commending ourselves to every man's conscience in the sight of God.

2 Corinthians 4:4 Whose minds the god of this age has blinded, who do not believe, lest the light of the gospel of the glory of Christ, who is the image of God, should shine on them.

Who is the god of this world? The devil! The devil hath blinded the minds (not the hearts) of them that believe not. Lest the LIGHT OF THE GLORIOUS GOSPEL OF CHRIST and you who are the IMAGE OF GOD, SHOULD SHINE UNTO THEM (SINNERS OF THE WORLD!) I believe we are to shine our light at gay weddings, to tree huggers and all the lost sheep because there minds are blinded but the heart is what my Jesus came to save and we are His vessels of transformation. As such we do not lose heart.

DO CHRISTIANS NEED COURTS

Light shines best through the transparency of our love for Jesus. Jesus never took anyone to court to transform their heart, or to protect His belongings. We will only lose in a court system. We lose because we are asking a court system to uphold our beliefs. We lose big time if they win because they are emboldened. If you win you keep your house and job but you haven't transformed anyone. The kingdom of God is not being established, but the kingdom of the devil has spread his hate through you for however long the court battle takes. For those of you who go to court and expect the courts to up hold your morals and beliefs as a Christian; you lose because you are putting your faith in the court not God. We cannot be vessel of God's love without faith. We prove our faith in our time of trial by standing firm in the power of His might. Please ask my Jesus to give you boldness and discernment.

I believe the love of Jesus flows best and is the most transparent to others when we surrender our cares to God, not the courts. We prove we are transparent by surrendering our problems to Jesus. You prove you are surrendered to Jesus by trusting Him. You prove you trust Jesus by believing in Him. You prove you believe Jesus by allowing Jesus to solve your problems, not the court. You prove you believe by the way you pray – that is, allowing Jesus to give you the answer and not some judge's ruling. I guess what I am trying to say is I believe in God being the

Supreme Being of Justice; I don't believe in the rulings of man's supreme court.

The steps to renewing your mind is believing, trusting, listening and surrendering all to Jesus. You receive them by asking Jesus into your heart. And as Jesus starts renewing your mind, your actions, your walk, and your thoughts will start to line up with the love of Jesus you allowed into your heart. We prove we believe by letting Jesus be our teacher, a trusted teacher will bring only truth and comfort. I believe in the truth of Jesus and the comfort of knowing Jesus loves you drives all fears away and this is why Jesus called it perfect love.

A life lived in the perfect love of Jesus is a life that will transform the lives of others; please do not hide behind your morals instead let them shine! Like I said, I start my day by asking God, "What are we going to do today?" I believe my focus is on Jesus not in lawyers, courts, and judges. I almost never get an answer to my question, but I know by faith God has an answer for me and He knows I will not try to make something happen on my own. I simply let the love of God flow. I have simply asked Jesus to be my very best friend and by faith I know Jesus loves me and I am His best friend. Knowing Jesus loves me is truly comforting. Living in the loving embracing comfort of Jesus gives me the strength to go into a sinner's house (gay contract) and allow Jesus to transform someone right before my eyes

> **John 14:31** But that the world may know that I love the Father, and as the Father gave Me commandment, so I do. Arise, let us go from here.

Before Jesus went to the cross, He told the apostles where He was going and what was about to happen. The willingness of Jesus to go through the trials He endured while on earth, the calmness of Jesus to take on the burden of the sins of the world, and the peace Jesus displayed before and during and after the trials prove beyond any doubt that Jesus was living in a relationship with His Father in heaven. The life of Jesus is so much more than most churches teach. We must take time from our busy schedule to hear His

186

voice, we must ask Jesus into our heart and then live from our heart. We read John 14:31 again:

John 14:31 But that the world may know that I love the Father, and as the Father gave Me commandment, so I do. Arise, let us go from here.

Jesus was answering questions before the apostles asked them. Jesus even gave the apostles the answer to the why questions. Like why do you have to die? Why do you have to suffer? Etc. When he said, "That the world may know that I go to my Father," Jesus wanted the apostles to know and see that all things are possible. Jesus wanted the world to know that He was just following commands from the Father when He said, "As the Father gave me commandment, and even so I do." Jesus knew what He was about to go through and I believe it is humanly impossible for us to endure what Jesus endured unless you live in relationship with Jesus, because then all things are possible.

Jesus said in John 14:31, "Arise, let us go hence." Jesus marched right into His own trial. Why are we so afraid to go to a gay wedding? We have the Savior of the world with in us. We cannot mess up, and we have the same relationship with Jesus as Jesus had with His Father. Fear should not even be in our thinking. Die to yourself and look at the opportunity to be an example of the love of Jesus to the world. Change one heart at a time. Now THAT'S MY JESUS AND HE LOVES FLOWING THROUGH US!

The photographer has an opportunity to be the love of Jesus to some gays. She knows Jesus loves her with His perfect love. She will have the peace and joy of Jesus inside her. She will be in total peace if she is not trying to make something good happen. Good will happen simply because she has surrendered to God and by surrendering to God, she has become a vessel of His perfect love. His love is her joy and her strength. The love of Jesus will flow through her and His love will transform them.

The kingdom of God operates in His perfect love without fear. In faith, she can take the pictures of the contract between them and plant some really big seeds of God's love. Knowing Jesus dwells inside her will enable her to be the love of Jesus. And Jesus will give her the strength and wisdom and seeds to plant.

My friend tried to change my mind again by saying, "Can you imagine Jesus receiving money for taking pictures of the contract?" For him, receiving money for taking pictures of the contract was condoning their contract. For him, this was tolerating the contract and Jesus would never tolerate a gay marriage or even a gay contract. I know Jesus would never tolerate this kind of behavior. I am not advocating, condoning, or tolerating this contract – I simply see this is an opportunity to show the heart transforming love of Jesus to others. We are not judging we are loving.

I know the will of the Father. I know what happened to whole cities that lived the gay lifestyle in the Old Testament. Jesus is right up front with how He deals with this kind of behavior. Before Jesus destroyed the city Jesus said to Abraham if you can find fifty good in that city I will spare it.

Genesis 18:23-33 And Abraham came near and said, "Would You also destroy the righteous with the wicked? Suppose there were fifty righteous within the city; would You also destroy the place and not spare it for the fifty righteous that were in it? Far be it from You to do such a thing as this, to slay the righteous with the wicked, so that the righteous should be as the wicked; far be it from You! Shall not the Judge of all the earth do right?" So the Lord said, "If I find in Sodom fifty righteous within the city, then I will spare all the place for their sakes." Then Abraham answered and said, "Indeed now, I who am but dust and ashes have taken it upon myself to speak to the Lord: Suppose there were five less than the fifty righteous; would You destroy all of the city for lack of five?" So He said, "If I find there forty-five, I will not destroy it." And he spoke to Him yet again and said, "Suppose there should be forty found there?" So He said, "I will not do it for the sake of forty." Then he said, "Let not the Lord be angry, and I will speak: Suppose thirty should be found there?" So He said, "I will not do it if I find thirty there." And he said, "Indeed now, I have taken it upon myself to speak to the Lord: Suppose twenty should be found there?" So He said, "I will not destroy it for the sake of twenty." Then he said, "Let not the Lord be angry, and I will speak but once more: Suppose ten should be found there?" And He said, "I will not destroy it for the sake of ten." So the Lord went His way as soon as He had finished speaking with Abraham; and Abraham returned to his place.

If no one was found righteous in the city, I believe that meant there was no hope for the city. Now we, the born again Christians can be the hope if we are not in fear. The people in that day were not born again because Jesus hadn't come yet. Our power is in our belief that Jesus defeated the devil, the power of Jesus in us if we simply believe.

Jesus wants us to be His voice of opposition to the gay lifestyle by simply being the love of Jesus – by trusting in the love of Jesus to flow through us. Jesus sees our belief in Him as hope for sinners. Jesus will bring the right words to us. Look at what Jesus did to the people who were defiling His Father's house.

> **Mark 11:15-17** So they came to Jerusalem. Then Jesus went into the temple and began to drive out those who bought and sold in the temple, and overturned the tables of the money changers and the seats of those who sold doves. And He would not allow anyone to carry wares through the temple. Then He taught, saying to them, "Is it not written, 'My house shall be called a house of prayer for all nations'? But you have made it a 'den of thieves.'"

Notice Jesus did not judge the men in the temple. Jesus simply threw them out! I believe Jesus will lead us and gives the answer and guidance to every situation or Jesus would not have asked us to follow. I will follow my Jesus by faith and walk in His love by faith and when prompted I will drive people out of the temple. The Bible goes on to tell us:

> **Mark 11:18-19** And the scribes and chief priests heard it and sought how they might destroy Him; for they feared Him, because all the people were astonished at His teaching. When evening had come, He went out of the city.

I asked you, *who told Jesus to leave the city?* There are times when people were going to kill Jesus and He disappeared among them. His Father is our Father if you believe. And our Father will protect us, just like He did for Jesus, for when we are born again we our His children and I believe my Father will transport me to safety if need be. I don't believe Jesus ever walked in fear. I believe Jesus had a great relationship with His Father and walked in the perfect love of His Father. I believe Jesus modeled that perfect love to us so I simply believe I am loved and protected because I am! Can you imagine Jesus telling His Father, "I'm afraid so I won't go to the gay contract because it won't look good for you Father if I go?" If you said no I can't see these words coming from my Jesus; I believe we are on the same page.

The first words of the prayer Jesus gave us are 'Our Father'. I have a Father. He sends His Holy Spirit to dwell in me and I believe He is with me always. I don't walk in fear because I know Jesus is always near. I walk in the comfort of knowing that Jesus came to set us free of worry (troubled at heart) and fear (being afraid). We are to walk boldly; knowing Jesus has put us Christians in the garden and is waiting for us to make it into Eden again. Jesus is in my heart so my heart will not be troubled and I will not be afraid.

John 14:26-27 But the comforter, the Holy Spirit, whom the Father will send in My name, He will teach you all things, and bring to your remembrance all things that I said to you. Peace I leave with you, My peace I give to you; not as the world gives do I give to you. Let not your heart be troubled, neither let it be afraid.

Jesus is telling us His Father will send us the Holy Spirit who will comfort us, and teach us and bring all things to your remembrance. He gives peace and takes away worry and fear. These are gifts of His love for us. Jesus gave these gifts to all of us knowing we will all sin and fall short of the mark. Jesus forgave us our sins before we even ask. Look how the love of Jesus forgives.

For a lot of people, forgiveness is the biggest stumbling block to knowing God. If your focus is on your pain, or who hurt you, or the blatant sin they are in; such as the gay lifestyle, your focus is not on Jesus. Jesus at the end of His earthly life said forgive them Father for they know not what they do. Jesus did not say for us to
190

hold their lifestyle against them, but we are to be an example of the love of Jesus to the sinners just as Jesus was. We are to march right into the sinner's house and be the love of Jesus to them. We are to forgive them for they know not what they do.

Jesus said this after He was being beaten for three days and all His friends deserted Him. If you are holding back on your forgiveness toward anyone, you need to read the book on forgiveness. The book is titled *Bible*, written to show us the inspired life of Jesus and forgiveness is on every page. We are to show forgiveness by the way we live, the way we walk and by the way we forgive.

Luke 23:34 Then Jesus said, "Father, forgive them, for they do not know what they do." And they divided His garments and cast lots.

Luke finished this Scripture by proving that Jesus left this world without owning any material possession – not even his clothes. Jesus is the ultimate giver, ultimate forgiver, the ultimate author, the ultimate teacher and most of all, the ultimate lover. I have the privilege of having Jesus as my ultimate best friend. Ask Him into your heart and let the transforming begin.

I know we are here to help the people who are lost and living in the ways of man by helping they find the Truth who will set them free. We set people free, first by forgiving them, for they know not what they do. We need to see them through the Eyes of Jesus, so we see their potential not there sin. Knowing we are walking in the love of Jesus is peace and Joy we share with everyone. From tree huggers to gay and lesbian sinners we need to forgive as Jesus forgives for there is only one judge and He will judge righteously.

Jesus knew His Father's love for him. Jesus was simply a vessel of His Fathers love to others. Jesus heard from His Father all the time. Jesus knew His Father's voice and discerned it. I believe we can walk in that same realm of understanding the will of the Father. I believe this is a time for hearing from my Father because I believe Jesus came and died for me to be able to commune with Him 24/7 and I will.

I have seen little mustard seeds of God's love transform people into the image and likeness God created us to be. Watching the love of Jesus flow into someone is beyond exciting – it is witnessing Jesus transforming a heart and we are all called to be His vessel by simply being the love of Jesus. I don't have a plan for my life, I don't have a plan for a big ministry but I believe I have everything I need for today. I believe when I pray Jesus hears me and Jesus has an answer for my prayer and I know by faith Jesus is the answer and Jesus has a plan for my life. My life is simple – Jesus loves me and I know it!

One more thought about the gay contract. I doubt very seriously these men would walk into a church building to hear the word of God. I doubt they would listen to anyone preach God's truth to them. I believe the world has hardened their hearts somehow. But let someone walking and living in the love of Jesus walk into their life; especially someone they invited and I believe that someone who lives in the realm of the transforming power of Jesus; will change their hearts as they watch the love of Jesus flow through them.

I believe in miracles. Jesus believed in miracles. The miracles of Jesus transformed hearts towards His Father, so we should all believe in miracles. I mean, by faith all things are possible, even the transforming of lifestyles.

Think about this for a moment. There are plenty of gay photographers around that could have been ask to do the contract? Why didn't these men ask a gay man to take the pictures of the contract? I believe the devil uses every opportunity to spread his hate and his fear to others. If we Christians back down the devil wins. If we go to court the devil wins, but when we stand firm in our faith in Jesus Christ we win! Please stand firm and believe!

Jesus said that He is truth, and I believe Him. How will sinners know they are sinning without the truth of Jesus in their life? We are commanded to boldly proclaim the truth to every creature. We are told not to judge, but we are able to recognize. Please read your Bible – it is the will of God that not even one of

His creations to perish. It doesn't say unless the devil has made them gay. I believe it is our job to carry out the will of our Father.

Ask yourself this question: If she says it is against my morals to do your wedding because they are gay, who do you think wins? Not God's team. In fact, we are giving them the (followers of the devil) the power to instill fear in us. We know the court (man's laws) sides with the gays in the past. So they are emboldened and we look like cowards. Sin is sin to Jesus. For example, Jesus saw Saul killing His followers and yet Jesus was not looking at Saul as a murderer. Jesus saw Saul's potential and transformed Saul into Paul.

Another example: Jesus never backed down because of what people might say about Him. Jesus knew in those days a tax collector was considered almost as bad as a murderer. Tax collectors were considered scum and no one of any stature would socialize with them. So why would Jesus go to a sinner's house to eat? Jesus went right into the tax collectors house – in fact, Jesus invited Himself into the tax collectors house. I believe Jesus gave us the perfect way to lead a man to repentance.

Luke 19:2-7 Now behold, there was a man named Zacchaeus who was a chief tax collector, and he was rich. And he sought to see who Jesus was, but could not because of the crowd, for he was of short stature. So he ran ahead and climbed up into a sycamore tree to see Him, for He was going to pass that way. And when Jesus came to the place, He looked up and saw him, and said to him, "Zacchaeus, make haste and come down, for today I must stay at your house." So he made haste and came down, and received Him joyfully. But when they saw it, they all complained, saying, "He has gone to be a guest with a man who is a sinner."

After being with Jesus a short time, Zacchaeus gave his heart to God and declared his transformed heart to everyone there.

Luke 19:8-10 Then Zacchaeus stood and said to the Lord, "Look, Lord, I give half of my goods to the poor; and if I have taken anything from anyone by false accusation, I restore fourfold." And Jesus said to him, "Today salvation has come to this house, because he also is a son of Abraham; for the Son of Man has come to seek and to save that which was lost."

We are to proclaim the Word of God to all, even if we are in a bathroom, taking a shower. We are here to seek and save the lost just like Jesus. We are Sons of God just like Jesus. We are here to bring salvation to the lost, just like Jesus. We are to be bold just like Jesus. I cannot picture in my mind Jesus taking pictures of a gay wedding but I cannot picture Jesus running from an invitation to go to the sinner's house and bring salvation. Jesus was never too moral to talk to a sinner. These gay men are lost because no one has proclaimed the good news of Jesus to them. I believe we should run to these opportunities and not form these opportunities.

If we use our morals to set standards to determine who we will talk to and who we will spend time with, I think we are missing the mark. Our morals should be on display, like our beliefs and like our walk with Jesus. A wise man once said, "Preach the Gospel of Jesus Christ 24/7 and if you have to, use words."

By going to the sinner's house, Jesus transformed the heart of Zacchaeus. There are many stories in the Bible that talks about Jesus transforming one heart at a time. I believe the most important heart Jesus wants to transform now is yours! The heart Jesus wants you to transform is the person next to you, even if the person next to you is gay. Jesus came to set us all free from the bondage of sin and there is no limitation on where or when and who.

The Love of Jesus on Display

I want to talk about the love of Jesus for a moment. A while ago, I was asked to go to the mountains here in California with a couple who were camping next to me. We were looking at the awesome splendor of God's work from a very high overlook, when I mentioned, "Do you know why God made all this?" They asked, "Why do you think God made all this?" I answered, "God did all this for me, so I personally could enjoy His work today. God did all this just for me and just for this moment." They looked at me like *you are conceited aren't you?* I said, "No. I am not conceited, I just know how much God loves me and I know for a fact God will create all this for me. When you realize God will do this and more just for you, then you are starting to realize how much God loves you. Jesus said nothing is impossible for us who believe in Him and coming into a realization of His love is the first step of knowing nothing is impossible for you too!"

Recently I had a desire to see some friends, Mathew and Heidi, whom I had met in Georgia. These friends now live in Oregon. On the way, I went to Redding, California for about a week. I knew Bill Johnson has a ministry and a church there. Arriving at the campground, I met the owners and sat in their office for a couple hours as Ron, the owner told me about his life. This man should be a poster child for forgiveness. The Joy of the Lord in him is so contagious. His life and circumstances would have been enough to break a person, but Ron's deep rooted love of the Lord allowed Him to rise above the circumstances and Jesus replaced the hurt in Ron with Joy.

After leaving the office, I drove to my site and hooked up my camper. While hooking up, I met Glen and Theresa, my new neighbors. After eating my dinner, I went over to talk to them. In just minutes it seemed like we were old friends.

I tell everyone about how Jesus always looks out for me. My friend Megan called from Canada and said she had something she wanted to send me. She knows Matthew and Heidi also and Megan was really happy to hear Matthew was coming to see me. I gave her the address for the campground and Megan said there would be a package coming the next day or so. Megan would not tell me what the package contained.

My friend Matthew came down from Oregon the next day. I introduced Matthew to Glen and Teresa and they enjoyed talking to him. In the afternoon, Matthew and I went to eat. Then we received a text message from Megan saying the package was delivered to my campsite. There seemed to be some urgency and a lot of excitement in Megan's voice so we hurried back to the campground.

I couldn't figure out what Megan had sent in the package, so there was excitement in my heart also. Megan had sent me and I-pad by Apple. If I was by myself when the iPad came, I probably could not even turn it on, let alone use it. I realized Jesus sent Matthew to me because he is a genius on the iPad. He taught me how to use it.

Megan was so happy to hear that the iPad arrived and that Matthew gave me some skill to use it. Matthew is so patient with me and is truly concerned that I understand how to use it. I'm sure I will use the iPad and it will become a great tool to help spread the word of Jesus Christ. I know Megan's heart and her love for Jesus transforms lives one heart at a time. The timing of this gift is working in the hearts of people around us also. Thank you Jesus, I love you too!

My new friends Glen and Theresa wanted to know why Megan would send you such a nice gift. I said, "I don't know other than she loves me and wanted me to have it." The next day, another package came and it was a good snack food to eat while learning the iPad. The second package blew their minds because it had to be packed in ice packs to arrive in eatable condition. I believe Megan was teaching the love of God to people she didn't know by being the love of God in ways she didn't even think about. A lot of people talk about how God will take a bad situation and turn it into something good if you let Him. I believe God uses every thought we have and every action we have, and God will turn the good into something even better. Open your heart to God by being simply tuned into what God has for you to do today.

I am sure when Megan had a desire to send me an iPad. She didn't pray and ask God to make sure other people were around to see this good deed she did so they might be impressed and know what a good person she is. When your heart is pure, your motives become pure and the results are purely in God's hands. Yes, God will turn good into better than good, if you let him. Megan makes her heart available to God every day. Make your heart available to God and watch God purify you. Watch as God bring joy into this world through you and watch the love of God transform the hearts of people you have never met. Isn't God the greatest!

God loves to magnify our good works. If Glen and Theresa ever met Megan, they will already know her as a great person who hears from God. Megan's heart is to be with God every day. I already knew Megan's heart, but now because of God magnifying her act of kindness towards Glen and Theresa, they now know her heart also. I have never met Megan's mom but I know she also has a big heart for the Lord.

I tell everyone I meet how I am blessed. I do not consider myself blessed because Megan sent me an iPad. I know I am blessed because I know how much Jesus loves me. I am blessed to have a relationship with the Creator of the world and I am blessed to know Jesus and I are on a first name basis. My self-worth is in my relationship to Jesus and not how many people love me and send me gifts. I appreciate Megan's heart and Mathew's heart and the heart of all those who loves me because all my friends have a relationship with Jesus and that makes them special to Jesus and me. Please put your trust in Jesus, the one who said He will never leave me or forsake you. Put your trust in Jesus and you can open your heart to be the love of Jesus to others knowing Jesus will never leave you or forsake you. Presents are nice, but they do not make or break my day. Presents bring momentary happiness, but knowing God loves you is Joy beyond understanding.

I believe knowing that Jesus loves you is the most important lesson you can ever learn. The love of Jesus is the gift of peace, joy, trust and faith. Having Jesus as your best friend is the answer to the troubles of this world, knowing Jesus lives inside you is peace and boldness, having a relationship with Jesus is being able to surrender to Him, knowing Jesus loves you is knowing Jesus has the answer. When we have a relationship with Jesus, we can channel His love to other people and change their hearts for Him.

I tell people not to pray to God with an answer in their prayer. Instead, pray to God, knowing God has the answer to your prayer. Faith pleases God, his Word says so. Surrendering all your problems to God is the peace that surpasses all our understanding. I want for my children and my loved ones to be in heaven with me someday. So I prayed "dear heavenly Father only you and Jesus can make my request happen so I rest knowing you hear my prayer and I rest knowing my loved ones will be in heaven with us someday. Thank you Father and Jesus for making my request happen and I love you too. In Jesus name I pray and I believe so I rest knowing my loved ones will be in heaven someday."

Hebrews 11:6 But without faith *it* is impossible to please *Him*, for he who comes to God must believe that He is, and *that* He is a rewarder of those who diligently seek Him.

When we pray to God and make suggestions as to how we want God to answer our prayer, we prove that we have not yet surrendered our problems to Him. We prove that we are still trying to figure out our own solutions and really we are asking God for help but we are telling God this is the way we want Him to help. Surrendering to God takes Faith. Praying to God without an answer is praying in Faith. Faith pleases God! Believe me, God has an answer to every problem here on earth and I believe God is waiting for someone to ask Him for His answer. I believe the way we surrender our problems to God is to pray without trying to figure out the answer we want from God. If we simply pray knowing God is the answer and has an answer for us, we are praying in faith and a prayer in faith gives us the peace that surpasses all understanding. Praying in faith is our proof to the world we know Jesus loves us. Paul and Silas simply sang praises to the Lord and they got an answer!

198

I believe the great people of Faith today do not get up every day trying to please God. I believe they get up surrendered to God and listen for His voice because they know by faith they please God. To be pleasing to God all we need is faith to simply listen for His voice and obey. Even if you do not hear anything from God at that moment, I encourage you to go about your day and by faith you will know if you are going the wrong way God will turn you around.

The apostles followed Jesus because His love was on display 24/7. Follow Jesus by putting your love on display 24/7. Do not hold back to protect you heart, simply believe Jesus will protect your heart and you are protected! Never fear to put the love of Jesus in on display, in fact you are His ambassador of love so go transform someone today by simply being His love on display.

Surrendering To God

Let us talk about surrendering to God for a moment. Surrendering to God should be easy, but without faith it is actually impossible for most people. For example, like repenting of sin, some people I meet think to themselves, "I like the sin I am in so why should I want to repent for something I like doing?" One person I met actually said, "I'm too young for a relationship with God. I want to sow my wild oats now and have some fun! Then, when God rescues me, I will have a wild testimony! Is his atatude right? I mean, why repent for something you are not going to change or even have a desire to change." Jesus covered this situation when He talked about there is a way that seems right to a man but the wages of sin is death. This situation might seem impossible to breakthrough if you are trying to change someone's heart in your own strength.

If you surrender the situation to God and simply pray knowing God knows the desire of your heart, you will rest and have peace knowing God heard your prayer and you will know in your heart God has an answer. Your prayer of faith will take the burden of their salvation off you and your faith in God will shine on them. The darkness of sin will flee when the light of faith in Jesus shines through your life of faith in God.

I believe this story is a good example of knowing God and loving God, but not being surrendered to God. In the *Joy of the Lord* book is a story called Fear. I met a lady who was told to read the fear teaching by someone. After reading about fear she realized how she was living in fear. She told me this story.

Lori's husband died shortly after the birth of their son. Their son, Billy, was born mentally challenged. Lori's health started to fail as she took on the responsibility to provide for her son's well-being. She worked two jobs, forty hours a week to keep them in housing and forty hours a week to pay for insurance protection to provide a good home for Billy in the event Lori died. Lori wanted the peace of mind to know if something happened to her, Billy would be placed in a really good home and provided for the rest of his life. After reading the fear teaching, Lori realized she was living in fear and had no peace or joy in her life. And because of fear, she realized she knew of God, but didn't personally know God.

Shortly after Lori's realization of the need to know God personally, she quit one of her jobs and started spending time getting to know God intimately and she spent time telling Billy about God. They were both learning and Billy responded to her love with love. Lori found renewed strength in a loving relationship with God. The peace of knowing God would look after her Billy if anything happened to her was miraculous. The time she spent focusing on Jesus instead of the problem allowed her to see fear is actually believing in the power of the devil and faith believes in the love and power of God.

Simply pray with faith, knowing God has an answer. When you do, peace, joy, and love of Jesus will overtake your life and its problems. Billy's terrible problems, his terrible anger and his whole life responded to the love of Jesus flowing through Lori, when Lori asked God into her heart and life by responding to the call of Jesus. Jesus is calling us all to His love and all we have to do is surrender our problems to Him. This is impossible unless you know for a fact the Creator of the universe loves you and wants nothing more than to spend time with you. Living in the Joy of the Lord is peace and peace is living knowing Jesus has the answer. Lori's life of faith in the Lord will change the hearts of people around her, not because of her preaching about God's love, but because she is now a walking vessel of His love. Ask God '*what are we going to do today*' and I bet you do not hear. No, I know you will not hear, work two jobs until you are exhausted.

Lori still doesn't know how Jesus will take care of Billy in the event she dies, but Lori knows by faith Jesus has a way of taking care of Billy and Lori is surrendered to "THE WAY, THE TRUTH AND THE LIGHT" knowing my Jesus is knowing Jesus will solve our problems!

The answer to the question 'Jesus, what are we going to do today' is always the same: Jesus just wants us to be a vessel of His never ending love.

Why are we working two jobs when faith in God moves mountains and faith comes by hearing the word of God? Are we trying to move the mountain by working two jobs? Don't try to tell God how to move the mountain, for in doing so we are not listening for the word from God. How can God build our faith if we are telling God how to solve the problem? Just be still and listen for the Word of God and believe God can move the mountain and God will make the mountain crumble into the sea.

I believe my Jesus is alive and well in this world. I have a desire in my heart to see more and more people turn to my Jesus as their source of Joy and love, and to become vessels of that joy and love to others. I believe Jesus will give more and more people the desire to turn to Him. I believe our simple act of kindness towards one another is being magnified by God for His glory. Our simple act of obedience is to listen for the answer from God instead of telling God how or what needs to happen. This simple change in our prayer life will allow God to flow through us and hearts will be transformed everywhere. Loving Jesus is easy to say, but knowing how much Jesus loves us is very hard to comprehend. Simply live to give glory to God by allowing the Glory of God to flow into a heart today.

Some people I know live to tell testimonies of what God is doing through them. If you want a great testimony, simply become the love of God to someone today. Don't try to make something great happen – just let God give you something great to do by simply listening for His voice. Make yourself available to Jesus and Jesus will flow through you. Life really is that simple. I love my Jesus and I know Jesus loves me! Thank you Jesus for transforming me.

HEARING FROM GOD

Discernment is very important. Sometimes, I am prompted to wait to hear from God before talking or praying for someone. Like the children in the wheel chairs I talked about earlier in this book. Sometimes I just call on the Lord and he shows off for me.

The other day I met a man named Dustin. Dustin needed a ride to Santa Monica, CA. From where we were, the drive would be about 120 miles. I told him I would take him. Dustin knew the drive was all the way through Los Angles and he told me thanks for the offer but it was too much to ask.

I insisted and Dustin said okay because he knew how difficult it would be to hitch a ride through Los Angles. After getting into my car, Dustin explained to me he is homeless, although He has a job. His job keeps him on the road and in motels all the time. Now, he has ten days off and he decided to go see his parents. To find our way to Santa Monica, Dustin used his smart phone. We started talking about my favorite and only topic: the love of Jesus and how His love affects our lives.

I drove for about ten minutes when Dustin noticed my gas gauge was on total empty. He said we better stop and get gas and I noticed he was almost panicking. I told him my gas gauge doesn't work. He asked me, "How do you know how much gas you have in your tank?" I smiled and answered him, "Most of the time I just try to remember when I got gas last and approximately how far I have driven. If I cannot remember I simply ask Jesus how much gas I have in my tank and Jesus makes my gas gauge work long enough for me to see how much gas I have left."

Dustin started laughing and said, "You asked Jesus to show you how much gas is in your tank and Jesus answers?" I said, "Yea, and Jesus will show me right now." So I asked, "Jesus, how much gas do I have in my tank?" and the gas gauge went up to a half a tank and then back to empty. Dustin saw the gas gauge register a half a tank and said, "I don't believe this!" Dustin was laughing very hard as I said, "Thank you Jesus for showing me how much gas I have!" Then Dustin said, "Do it again! That was so cool!" So, I asked Jesus to make the gas gauge work again and immediately the gauge registered half a tank and then went back to empty. We were both laughing and continued talking about my Jesus.

The trip went really fast. It seemed like just minutes and we were there. Dustin told me to pull into a parking garage where we could park for three hours free. He then bought us a large pizza and we went to a park by the beach to eat. There, we met a homeless man who ate half our pizza himself. We even bought him a bottle of water to drink. The homeless man started talking and talking for about an hour. His ramblings were hard for me to figure out, but he was definitely telling us something hard to explain. He said he could see into the spirit world.

Before we left him, he allowed us to pray for him. I naturally ask God to give him discernment as to who he was listening to and to help his mind stay focused on Jesus. Dustin prayed a beautiful prayer over him and told him about shelters with free food in the area.

We went for a walk on a long pier. Some people there begged for money by playing music and some made money making flowers which they sold. During this time, Dustin called his dad and left him a message. Dustin told his dad he had ten days off work and wanted to visit. As night time came, Dustin looked up motels on his smartphone because he hadn't heard from his dad. I took Dustin to the motel he chose which was about 40 miles away. On the way to the motel, Dustin saw a gas station and said to me, "I want to buy you some gas." I replied, "I don't think I need any gas yet." Dustin started laughing, he saw the gauge was still reading empty and ask me to ask God how much gas was in my tank now. Jesus showed me immediately I had one fourth of a tank left and immediately the gauge went back to empty. The joy of watching God show off is wildly joyful. I love you Jesus!

We went to the motel where Dustin got the best price. There we said goodbye for now and I started back to the campground which was 122 miles away according to my GPS. I did get gas and the trip went very fast. The next day, Dustin called and said he was at his brother's house for a visit. I was very happy for him and we talked about Jesus for an hour and a half. I tell everyone that Jesus wants to be in our life and in every detail of our life. Jesus even tells me how much gas I have. I love you Jesus, but I love knowing YOU love me more! Yes! Your love for me blows me away all the time.

The love of Jesus gives us more joy in ways we cannot understand. When Jesus made my broken gas gauge work in front of Dustin, this simple act of kindness from Jesus showed Dustin Jesus is real and really in our details if we just call on Him.

A couple months later I was speaking in a church and told the gas gage story to the congregation there. After the service was over a man came up to me and ask me "where is that in the bible Ron; I didn't understand his question so he clarified it. He asks where in the bible does Jesus say He will tell you how much gas you have in your tank?" I said I don't know a pacific scripture where says Jesus will tell me how much gas I have in my tank. So I said out loud for him to hear. "Jesus where in the bible did you tell us how much gas is in our tank? Immediately I heard from Jesus this scripture

Mat 10:30 But the very hairs of your head are all numbered.

I believe Jesus is telling us if He cares enough to count the hairs on our head; Jesus cares enough to tell you how much gas is in your tank. I said I was married to my precious Jenny for forty years six months sixteen days and three hours and I loved her with all my heart but not once in all those years did I love her enough to even attempt to count the hairs on her head. I believe in this scripture Jesus is telling us He is in every detail of our life.

Actually, there is another gas gauge story that happened when I was in Redding, CA. Earlier this year, Matthew and I went to eat with Glen and Theresa one night. And on the way back to the campground, Matthew noticed my gas gauge on empty. I told Mathew how Jesus makes my gauge work and Jesus made it work for Mathew to see also. It was a great night. I think it is amazing to see the joy Jesus brings into our lives when we just ask Him into our lives.

Jesus is in our details if only we let Him. Please let Jesus into your heart. Listen for his voice and ask for discernment and you will have it. Jesus said faith comes by hearing the words of God in our heart. Hearing God in our heart will transform us into the image and likeness of Jesus. There really is no better place to be.

Surrender all your cares to God and pray knowing God has the answer already. My discernment tells me that when I pray, if I am suggesting to Jesus how he might handle a problem for me then I have not surrendered the problem to him because I am still trying to figure out how to handle the problem myself. Now, I simply thank God that He walks with me and my problems are already solved, right down to how much gas is in my tank. You know already Jesus is my best friend, but don't worry, I'm into sharing.

Jesus, what are we going to do today?

I'm hearing, "Go set some captives free." Now that is a plan and that's my Jesus!

I love my Coffee Time With Jesus. My gauge may say empty but I'll never run short of time to spend with my Jesus because I will spend eternity with Him. Knowing where and who I will spend eternity with gives me the peace only Jesus can give. Having joy of Jesus now and knowing that I am loved by the Creator of the universe is beyond my understanding! And I simply believe in Jesus and I have His love dwelling in me now.

Transforming the world, one heart at a time is a piece of cake when you simply let Jesus be Jesus. Knowing Jesus has the answer to our prayers and all we have to do is be willing vessels of His love. Simply let Jesus plan your day, by knowing Jesus has a purpose for your life. I meet people who have no purpose in life except for having fun and they think they are having fun! They can be having fun and in a split second be mad to boiling. They really don't understand fun will never turn into joy, but the Joy of the Lord will turn joy into fun.

TALENTS

In closing, I want to talk about the talents God has given each one of us. We will stand before Jesus for judgment someday and I believe Jesus will ask us about our talents and did we multiply them. Our talent is to be the free flowing love of Jesus on the earth today. No other accomplishment on earth will compare to being the representative of God, ask God into your heart and let the Joy begin.

1 Peter 4:8 And above all things have fervent love for one another, for "love will cover a multitude of sins."

I believe the love Jesus has for us is so strong that it will cover the multitude of our sins. The love Jesus has for us has forgiven us our sins. Jesus is talking about forgiveness. We are to believe in the fervent love Jesus has for us so we can have a fervent strong love toward all.

1 Peter 4:9 *Be* hospitable to one another without grumbling.

Love one another without complaining is not a suggestion. I believe we are to forgive without limitations. We are to forgive as we are loved by God. Love is forgiving and removing the punishment of sin as far as the east is from the west. Perfect love can do that and Jesus wants us to have His perfect love now.

I believe in Jesus when He said *above all things have fervent charity among yourselves.* I believe that is possible when we know the heart of God. From the charity of God, our hearts will desire to experience God intimately. The desire to receive the love of God in your heart will replace the desire for sin. I hope you understand that sin of all kinds will run away as fast and as completely as you seek to know God intimately. What I'm trying to say, "I don't fight sin anymore because I have replaced my desire for sin with a desire to know Father God and Jesus." The more intimately I desire and seek this relationship, the closer I walk with my Jesus, the less the things of the world hold me captive such as unforgiveness and worldly possessions. I am free to be the love of my Jesus and knowing the love of Jesus flows through me is true excitement, freedom to love others, Joyfulness and peace.

1 Peter 4:10 As each one has received a gift, minister it to one another, as good stewards of the manifold grace of God.

We are the stewards of the gift of God's love (grace) for we received God's grace freely so freely we give the same one to another. Ask Jesus for His heart and mind and eyes and Jesus will spoon feed you and transform you until one day you notice people looking at you differently and asking, "What happened to him?" My son, Jason told me, "You know dad, you are not the same dad that raised me." I told my son Jason, "Jesus will transform you if you let Him by seeking Him above all else."

1 Peter 4:11 If anyone speaks, *let him speak* as the oracles of God. If anyone ministers, *let him do it* as with the ability which God supplies, that in all things God may be glorified through Jesus Christ, to whom belong the glory and the dominion forever and ever. Amen.

There is a devil and he will tell you how stupid you are and he will tell you, you are not worthy. But here we read that if any man speak, let him speak as the oracles (the words of my God and the love of my God). If any man minister as Jesus ministered let him do so, as of the ability which God giveth to each one of us.

I have heard some pretty lofty preachers teach for hours and when they were done, I thought to myself, "What did he say? What was his point, to whom was he talking?" I am sure there are people who understood the preacher perfectly. I believe his message was beyond me. That doesn't make me stupid or him smart; it simply means I didn't understand his message.

On the other hand I have heard the Word of the Lord come through people who did not seem learned. Never put yourself down. Give your heart to the Lord and watch Him use you to transform hearts. For Jesus will use you at whatever education level you are. You will see miracles of love and wonder how did Jesus do that?

Only the devil will tell you that you don't have what God needs. You want to send the devil packing! Just start to focus on God and believe that you are a child of God! And as the child God, He would leave the ninety and nine to go find you and rejoice over finding you. Start walking and talking about the life of Jesus and you will give glory to God through Jesus Christ who paid the price for us. Jesus did not pay for you because you are too stupid to be used by Jesus and loved by Jesus. Never put yourself down. You are the child God rejoices over!

Praise God and give Him dominion over your life, by simply asking, "Jesus, what are we going to do today?" The love of Jesus is forever and ever AMEN. The love of Jesus is new every day so tell Jesus you are available and be available to receive His love every day! Remember that you are His beloved child.

1 Peter 4:12 Beloved, do not think it strange concerning the fiery trial which is to try you, as though some strange thing happened to you

Remember Alyssa in the story above? Her trial was upon her and her heart of love for the Lord shines. Your trial is upon you so let your heart speak the love of Jesus to all! Your love will shine and you will prove you have faith. Trials are not strange for Christians, but trials are how we show the world we are Christians. Please seek to bring Glory to God by being an example of His love and let Jesus write your testimony in Hebrews 11. Bring glory to God by being the glory of God. I actually pray for my trial because I know the bigger the trial the more glory my Jesus can receive from it.

1 Peter 4:13 But rejoice to the extent that you partake of Christ's sufferings, that when His glory is revealed, you may also be glad with exceeding joy.

I love my Jesus so much! I know by being a partaker of the sufferings, I can be a giver of His glory and when the Glory of Jesus is revealed through our trials, we will be glad also as our Father in Heaven is glad to see our belief in Him manifested and we all – Jesus, Father God, Holy Spirit and I will have exceeding Joy.

1 Peter 4:14 If you are reproached for the name of Christ, blessed are you, for the Spirit of glory and of God rests upon you. On their part He is blasphemed, but on your part He is glorified.

When you are insulted because of your love of Jesus Christ, be happy for you have the spirit of God rests upon you. I know for a fact Jesus lives in me and I choose to focus on Jesus living in me. I rest for I know He will shine His Glory on us the believers. Jesus wins every time so let not your heart be troubled.

1 Peter 4:15 But let none of you suffer as a murderer, a thief, an evildoer, or as a busybody in other people's matters.

We are not to take on the burdens of a murderer, a thief, an evildoer, or a busybody who meddles in others affairs by taking on their pain and offering only sympathy. We are the light! We are to be compassion and the way to shine sinners towards our Lord and Savior Jesus Christ. We will be a giver of hope in the storm, a light in darkness and a Christian in this world.

Remember in the storm that Jesus didn't give sympathy to the apostles. Jesus did not say, "It is okay, peace, be calm, beg me for help, I fell your pain, Pray and you will be okay. Now have a nice day guys!" No! Jesus took control and told the storm to go away. We are not partakers of problems, neither are we the answer to sinner's problems. We give them hope by being the light of Jesus and showing them the compassion of Jesus, (commanding change if need be) and by bring the one who has the answer and is the answer. JESUS IS OUR SOURCE AND JESUS IS THE ANSWER!

1 Peter 4:16 Yet if anyone suffers as a Christian, let him not be ashamed, but let him glorify God in this matter

If someone slanders your name and brings suffering to you because of your Christian beliefs, like mine on how to help gays, I will not be ashamed. I will stand in faith. I have heard from my Jesus and I know my stand of faith brings glory to my Father God in heaven. Faith pleases God and our faith brings Him glory on this behalf.

1 Peter 4:17 For the time has come for judgment to begin at the house of God; and if it begins with us first, what will be the end of those who do not obey the gospel of God?

We are to walk in faith. We are to talk in faith. We are children of God by faith and we are to hear by faith and have our being in Faith of our loving God. We ought to shine the love of Jesus to all! And thank God we have no responsibility to judge others for in doing so, we only judge ourselves. We are to love others as Jesus loves us even in our sins, knowing we are not the judge takes all the pressure off us so we are free to love others. Jesus, the all-knowing One is the judge and His judgment will begin with us, His followers and we need to pray for the ones that obey not the gospel of God.

1 Peter 4:18 Now "If the righteous one is scarcely saved, Where will the ungodly and the sinner appear?"

Here we are to realize that yes, even the righteous may only be scarcely saved because the temptation to fall away from my Jesus is great. The sucking of the material things of this world, the sucking of pornography to lure men and women away from God, the sucking of contracts instead of marriages, the sucking of drugs to find some peace out side a relationship with God all these things suck us off the narrow path if we don't keep your hearts focused toward the Lord. Television, news, porn, drugs, internet, movies, material things, etc. will suck you away from the love of Jesus if we are not focused on Him. For the ungodly will appear in all those places and he, the devil will suck the life out of you with sin which can also be in the form of fear, unforgiveness, etc. The devil will steal the love of God in us by consuming our time, our energy and our life on earthly things which are brought into our living room through foolishness and humor. Simply focus on Jesus and His joy of the Lord is yours now and forever.

1 Peter 4:19 Therefore let those who suffer according to the will of God commit their souls to Him in doing good, as to a faithful Creator.

Here we see that we will suffer trials according to the will of God. Not everyone on earth loves God the way we Christians do. Not everyone on earth has even heard of the perfect love of Jesus.

It is our job to tell them in action and word just what Jesus did. We will suffer injustice, but during our trial, we, as Christian are to keep our focus on Jesus and look to the keeping of their hearts (perpetrators). No one has ever displayed this more then Jesus at the cross

Yes, even when Jesus was being nailed and hung on the cross for a long and painful death, Jesus prayed for the perpetrator's souls. Jesus did not ask His Father why – Jesus just saw His cross as a way to prove His faith in His Father and at the same time give the world an example of the perfect love of His Father flowing through Him. Jesus did not go to a gay contract to take pictures, but I believe Jesus when He said go to the ends of the earth and preach my life and my perfect love to them.

We are to bless those that persecute us for through them we have a chance to prove we know we are loved by God. We should rejoice knowing our name is in the Book of Life. The apostles rejoiced after being beaten because they counted it as glory to suffer for the name of Jesus. Jesus brought glory to God our Father by going through the trial He went through.

Jesus is the keeper of my soul. I have surrendered my heart to Him. In my trial, I pray to keep my mind focused on my Creator and not the trial. I pray that I can forgive them Father for they know not what they are doing. I pray I can and will pray for my persecutor that his soul be saved. I pray I can bring glory to God every single day of my life and I know I can because I have the love of Jesus in me and so I know Jesus makes all things possible for me. Jesus said so and I believe.

I believe all things are possible when we focus on Jesus and discern our thoughts. Discernment is so important. I know Jesus had great discernment and so I ask God for the discernment He gave Jesus. I believe Father God is no respecter of persons so what Father God did for Jesus He will do for me. I ask Jesus for the discernment of voices I hear. I only want Jesus in me and Jesus gives me the desires of my heart; so I am free, I am His and most of all I know He loves me.

WHY DO WE NEED DISCERNMENT?

I am camping in Las Vegas right now. I came to visit some friends that live here. I am so joyful I have my Jesus living inside of me because after being here a day or two, if I was not routed in the love of Jesus I believe this place could remove all hope I have for the world.

I read a story last night about how Las Vegas is embracing the porn industry. To the leaders in this town, porn is just another way to bring money and jobs into the area. The quest for money and power is so overwhelming in this town. Those who are weak in the Spirit are drawn here by a chance to make it big if they win. I know they the gamblers her are weak in the spirit and do not have discernment of spirits because no one in the kingdom of God would tell you happiness is yours forever if you win or make big in Las Vegas. Who are these people listening to? I wonder if they have ever been told about discernment.

Please pray for the people in government to come into a close and lasting relationship with you and I – that is a true Christian walking in the love of Jesus. Their hearts will hear the love of Jesus coming through you. Their minds will be transformed and our world will be forever transformed. Yes, I have Jesus in me and so I have hope for the people of this town also.

I pray for discernment for all these people. My heart is suffering according to the will of God to watch who these people are listening to (devil) but my heart is joyful knowing I have an answer as long as I stay faithful to my Creator who is my loving God. I make myself available to my Jesus so I am the solution, not the problem and Jesus gives me the answer every day. He has a tremendous love for me. All the momentary happiness of earthly goods will not suck my mind of my loving Jesus.

I focus on Jesus and I see the momentary happiness of Las Vegas as useless as the flashing lights of Las Vegas. I did not go into a casino but I was told about the bright lights and how after a while you cannot tell if it is day or night. I love to talk about discernment because it is so important and so needed here in Las Vegas, I met people happily telling me to go into a casino where you cannot even discern something so simple as to know if it is day or night.

213

The campground I am in has 8 foot high concrete walls and 3 feet high bob-wired fence on top of the walls to keep thieves out. The campground also has 24-hour security at the entrance to keep the beggars out. Every subdivision I saw was built with walls and of them with bob-wire for security.

I thought about the two worlds we live in. I choose Jesus with His joy and His love and no boundaries needed, or I could be sucked into the world of artificial happiness and light, with no hope except to steal or beg. For me, the hard part to figure out is the draw for people to happily come here knowing they have a 99% chance they will lose everything. Some people I meet are proud of the fact they are disciplined enough to know when to stop loosing; before they loose everything. I wonder how there conversations go around the dinner table with there children and grandchildren. Aren't we great we only lost this much bet we had fun.

Las Vegas is advertised as the city of excitement. I think Las Vegas is a city of hell and the real thieves own the casinos. Even the strip clubs have more morals then the casinos. I mean, at least you know you are going into sin at a strip club. The casinos try to hide your sin of greed and lust for money with bright lights and excitement. Las Vegas is a city of deceit, full of sin, full of hard times and full of lust of all kinds. If you want to see the real Las Vegas, just drive a block or two off the strip. Every state in the union has a capital. I think the capital of hell is Las Vegas.

I stayed here a week. I visited my friends who have chosen to live here. I know my time here was fruitful and so I am joyful knowing not even the glitter of Las Vegas can stop the love of Jesus. I thank God for His love for me and His gift of discernment. I pray for discernment for all the people of Las Vegas and for the people who willingly come here. Thank You Jesus for your love for me and allowing me to be your light in this darkness.

Now back to 1 Peter 5:1:

1 Peter 5:1 The elders who are among you I exhort, I who am a fellow elder and a witness of the sufferings of Christ, and also a partaker of the glory that will be revealed

We are to call upon the elders for help and in doing so we will exhort them. We are to become an elder for we are all the witnesses of the sufferings of Jesus Christ. By being a witness of the sufferings of Jesus who never complained and even took on the sufferings willingly, we too are to tell the world of His love willingly and willingly take on our suffering for in doing so we can bring glory to our loving Father God.

We are to pick up our own cross and lay down our life. Doing so, we become followers of Jesus Christ. By doing so, we can give Glory to God our Father through Jesus by simply believing we are the difference here today as Jesus was the difference then, now and forever. We have Jesus! We have our answer! I don't try to figure out how to make a difference in this world because I know the "I am" lives inside of me so I am the difference Jesus made me to be.

Life is amazing! We have God who sent His Son to reap more Sons. The life of His Son tells us that we also can make a difference in this world. Our source is from the One who said He cannot lie. Then, we have a devil who tells us to give up, that you cannot make a difference anyway, so go, just play, enjoy life, spend your money on yourself, buy toys, make a big splash, go to the casino, you are important etc... I tell you, choose well! The difference is living in heaven or hell now and forever.

1 Peter 5:2 Shepherd the flock of God which is among you, serving as overseers, not by compulsion but willingly, not for dishonest gain but eagerly

Feed the flock of God by being and living the word of God. See the big picture as Jesus sees it. We don't rule over others with laws and constraints, but rather being a vessel of the love of God. You know you freely received, so give willingly! Be the love of Jesus to all and all will be transformed. The devil makes us look at the problem, but when we focus on Jesus we see the solution and the solution is Jesus in us, with Jesus we are a team and Jesus makes all things possible through us.

1 Peter 5:3 Nor as being lords over those entrusted to you, but being examples to the flock

We will not change the world through the power of the law or with new creative laws against such things as porn and gambling and the rest of the sins of the world. In Genesis, we read that we have power and authority over all the earth except fellow men. Laws are over our fellow men, with laws come judgments, but with the love of Jesus we have transformations, no jails, no judgment.

We will change men by changing their hearts. And the way to change hearts for good is through the love of Jesus. We will see big changes in the world by transforming the hearts of the ones promoting these sins. Jesus told us to focus on Him and the problem is solved. We need to know that Jesus has an answer. We need to focus on Jesus who gave us an answer. The answer is "Don't lord over others, don't argue with others, instead we are to be examples to the flock." Just be an example of the love of my Jesus to the flock and let God bring the increase. We are not to lord over people – we simply become the perfect love of Jesus to the flock.

1 Peter 5:4 And when the Chief Shepherd appears, you will receive the crown of glory that does not fade away.

We walk in the love and faith that our Chief Shepherd shall appear and I know He will. We walk knowing our job is to transform the heart of the one in front of us right now because when Jesus was here on earth, He did not take on the responsibility of the problems of the world. Jesus changed the problems of the world by transforming the world, one heart at a time. Remember in the days to come, our Shepherd will appear in Glory. I believe His question to us will be, "Did you transform someone's heart by the way you lived?" Jesus gave us the path. Jesus is the light on the path and Jesus gave us the tools and the best gift of all – Jesus gave us His love.

Years ago, our Heavenly Father saw the problems in the world. He sent His Son to transform the world. Father God didn't have his Son take over the world by force. Jesus didn't take over one country or even one city by force. Jesus did not have or need wealth. Jesus never ran for a government position! Jesus simply lived the love of His Father. Jesus simply did what He saw His Father do. The teachings of Jesus are still impacting the world today because He only did what He saw His Father do.

I believe we should have the same impact on the world by only doing what we saw our Jesus do. For most people, this simple plan is just too simple. For some reason, I see this simple plan is the only plan. This simple plan was good enough for my Jesus and it is surely good enough for me.

The other day, I was talking to a young couple. I told them that someday I am going to see the Heavens open up and I will hear the thunderous voice of my Father in heaven say, "This is my beloved son Ron in whom I am well pleased!" They looked at me like, "You sure are arrogant aren't you?" To which I replied, "No. I am not conceited or arrogant at all. This is my goal and I believe it should be your goal. Jesus said that He is no respecter of persons so what my Father God did for His Son Jesus, He will do for His Son Ron and all of us. Just simply believe like a child and you will hear from Jesus what your part in His simple plan is.

This is the simple plan. Transform the world one heart at a time.

After delivering the one heart at a time message in church, a man came up to me and said "you know your message is great and I can tell you fell very adamant about it. He said the problem is it is just too late. America is going to hell in a hand basket and your message will not stop it." I looked at him and said, you know Father God is the supreme being of the universe and when He saw the world going to hell in a hand basket 2000 plus years ago; what did He do about it? If you are thinking He sent His son you are right. One person transformed the world and now Father God has sent us as His ambassadors. We are His sons and we have a choice to believe or not to believe.

Jesus asks before He left "when I return will I find Faith on the earth?" I believe to do nothing except complain takes no faith. I believe when Jesus comes back He should find us doing the

Kingdom work He prepared us to do. He told us to tell the sinners and to tell everyone the kingdom of God is at hand. I believe if we want to be pleasing to God we better be doing what he commanded us to do when He comes back. I have peace and joy in my heart because I know Jesus lives their and for me all things are possible. The faith of a mustard seed will transform the world.

Jenny, Ron and Jesus will love you now and forever!

Jesus is my best friend and He wants to be your best friend also.

Become the love of Jesus by simply letting the love Jesus has for you become you.

Jesus wants you to be part of His simple plan. Now, you know your call is to focus on Jesus and in doing so you can be the perfect love of Jesus to all. Transform this world, one heart at a time! I believe the simple plan is the perfect plan.

I know I am loved by Jesus. Do you?